Rebecca Lang's
SOUTHERN ENTERTAINING
for a New Generation

REBECCA LANG'S
SOUTHERN ENTERTAINING
for a New Generation

REBECCA D. LANG

CUMBERLAND HOUSE
NASHVILLE, TENNESSEE

Published by
Cumberland House Publishing
431 Harding Industrial Drive
Nashville, Tennessee 37211

Cover design: JulesRulesDesign
Cover photograph and color insert photographs: Bill Jayne, Something Different
Photography
Photo stylist: Rebecca Lang
Assistant food stylists: Adeline Craig, Martin Lai Tyam, Julie Roseman, M. Jill Harris,
Jennifer Bannon, Beth Hudson, Cynthia Freeman, Belinda Matonak, Natalie Zschiesche
Wine pairing and information: Donald Hackett
Text design: Mary Sanford

Library of Congress Cataloging-in-Publication Data
Lang, Rebecca D., 1976-
  Rebecca Lang's Southern entertaining for a new generation / Rebecca D. Lang.
     p. cm.
  ISBN 1-58182-388-6 (hardcover)
  1. Entertaining. 2. Cookery, American—Southern style. 3. Menus. I. Title.
  TX731.L335 2004
  642'.4—dc22

                                   2004009898

Printed in Canada
1 2 3 4 5 6 7—10 09 08 07 06 05 04

This book is dedicated to my grandmother, whom we called "Tom." We talked often of writing a book together and in a way, we have. Many of her recipes grace these pages as well as some of her insights in the kitchen. She taught me much of what I know about food, love, and life.

I will miss her always.
Sally Claudia Adair Thomas, 1902–2003

Contents

MORNING

Brunch for a Bunch / 27

Down-Home Breakfast / 37

Fruit Fantasy / 45

Sweet Sweet Breakfast / 55

NOON

High Noon / 65

A Crowd for Sunday Dinner / 73

Soup, Salad, and Sandwiches / 83

Fresh Southerner's Luncheon / 91

Acknowledgments

I want to thank my husband, Kevin, for providing me with never-ending moral support and encouragement. Throughout the writing of this book, he successfully and cheerfully played the roles of business advisor, editor, confidant, and countless others. He was my best taste-tester and a great resource for determination.

My career would not be possible without my parents, Mandy and William Dopson, who always made sure I had the best education and experience to take me where I wanted to go. I am forever grateful for the emphasis they place on family tradition and recipes. Constantly they worked hard to ensure my undertakings were meaningful. They have enabled me to accomplish all the things I've wanted to do.

My sister, Natalie, has always been my biggest cheerleader (and provider of props). She's driven hours to watch me teach and has tested quite a few recipes. Not only is she the best hostess I know, but she is also the epitome of the Southern woman. My husband's parents gave me a gift that made writing this book much easier: a new computer. They have always been very supportive in all of my endeavors. I am very thankful for their endless generosity.

Donald Hackett, of Sherlock's Wine Merchant, provided superb wine pairing information for this book. He's been a good friend to me and a priceless wine consultant to thousands. His pairings have always made my food taste even better.

I am indebted to my food stylists Adeline Craig, Cynthia Freeman, Martin Lai Tyam, Julie Roseman, M. Jill Harris, Jennifer Bannon, Beth Hudson, Natalie Zschiesche, and Belinda Matonak. They taught me what teamwork and a love of cooking can create. This winning combination of personalities resulted in an unforgettable photography experience. Bill Jayne's creativity and photography inspired me. His cheerful attitude and friendly persona made him a pleasure to work with.

Mary Moore and Cooley Fales of The Cook's Warehouse in Atlanta assisted in so many aspects of this book. Over dinner, they suggested I write a book about entertaining. They also loaned me the use of the beautiful kitchen on the cover and in several of the photographs. My career has grown exponentially as a direct result of their support. The Cook's Warehouse staff provided valuable assistance with props, equipment, and cooking tips. My kitchen is a better place because of them.

A warm thanks to Nathalie Dupree, who provided the start to my culinary career years ago. Her advice and mentoring shaped my cooking and directed my career path.

Dick Parker not only led me to my publisher, but also provided me with advice every step of the way. He made it possible for a book that was just an idea to actually come out on paper. His publishing experience was an invaluable component to this book.

My best friend, Natalie Zschiesche, has cooked in my hour of need and has truly been an inspiration to me in and out of the kitchen. Jennifer Jaax and Mara Hammond ensured I was dressed beautifully for the cover. They unknowingly have become my stylists as well as wonderful friends. I appreciate their tremendous support and much needed laughter. My supper club has been a source of support and encouragement when I needed them most.

Mary Sanford, my talented editor, has made this process a pleasure every step of the way. She is such a fantastic asset to Cumberland House it's beyond words. I appreciate her input, guidance, and months of long hours editing and designing. This book is an eye-catching collection of recipes because of her.

Chris Bauerle, accounts manager for Cumberland House, eased my transition into the realm of publishing. I'll never forget his call informing me, "I think we have a book." It's something I'd waited to hear for a long time.

Introduction

We Southern women have been forced by the ever-growing global economy to become just as fast-paced as our counterparts in the North. The days of sipping mint juleps on the porch are long gone, and in many cases so are the porches. Although we may slave over our computers eight hours a day, we still have an innate need to entertain and be hospitable. It's a characteristic that forms at the instant of conception.

Many of us grew up with mothers who were just as busy as we are. When both parents work and three kids have to be at softball and soccer practice at the same time, who has time to pass down family recipes? Thanks to growing up in a small town with little to do, I had time to learn to cook from two superbly wise women. Luckily, in my family, recipes are just as important as photo albums. My grandmothers were two of the greatest chefs who ever lived. No, they didn't go to culinary school or cook for a living, but they were both fantastic in the kitchen.

Somewhere along the way, my grandmothers' names of Sara and Claudia were replaced with shorter and easier names for children to pronounce. Even after all the grandkids were grown, the names stuck. My paternal grandmother, Sa, perfected grits and fried fish. I remember her cooking grits all day in preparation for one of her famous fish fries. (In South Georgia, grits are always served with fried fish.) Her macaroni and cheese has been my favorite comfort food all my life. Her sweet tea could have taken the place of dessert as it barely flowed from her milk-glass pitcher. Tom, my maternal grandmother, was a free spirit who mastered biscuits, fried chicken, and almost everything else Southern. She cooked up until the time she was ninety-nine years old. God blessed me with two wonderful grandmothers to guide me through the kitchen and the world.

Every Sunday, lunch was the equivalent of what most would call a dinner party. Each dish was presented on a platter, while sweet tea was poured at the very last minute to prevent the ice from melting and diluting the near syrupy liquid. We often had fried chicken, creamed corn, homemade biscuits, squash and onions, potato salad, deviled eggs, sliced tomatoes in the summer, and whatever fruit was in season stuffed into a pie. One hour after lunch, you could find us all fast asleep in my grandmother's living room. It must have been the sudden rise in our blood pressures.

I grew up loving food so much that hunger pains often sent me into the kitchen. My mom called me the "baby bird" of the family because I was never full. I still live for great food and all the joys of preparing it. Food is what brings families, or should bring them, around the table each night. It draws old friends together for a long lunch. Most of all, food manages to be one of the few things that make us stop our busy lives for a few moments and partake in an enjoyment with those around us.

That's why I love to host parties of any kind. Be it a baby shower, an afternoon fiesta, or even my supper club, I am in heaven as a hostess. Inviting my friends over to share a meal is what I truly love. I get so excited about having guests that I sometimes choose the plates and platters weeks in advance. (My husband feels this may be some type of disorder.)

I often found that my guests were mystified by the fact that a young woman could successfully have a dinner party with no caterers. The more often this happened, the more I wanted to find a way to impress upon young adults how easy it is to entertain with just a little prep work done ahead of time. I hope this book does just that and helps you to entertain with confidence and grace.

Many of the recipes you'll find inside these pages have been in my family for generations. I cooked with my grandmothers until I could make biscuits with my eyes closed. There's no need to go to your local "meat and three" for good fried chicken anymore. From the recipes for cakes to the famous Apricot Puffs, I could tell a story about each and every one of them. For those of you who haven't spent a great deal of time in the kitchen, these recipes make becoming a fantastic Southern cook attainable. My instructions are easy to understand for any skill level. I hope I've taken the intimidation out of the Southern kitchen.

I've included several hints and tips that make cooking and entertaining easier. To make shopping for a party more manageable for busy schedules, a grocery and staple list is included with each menu. Wine suggestions are offered for most menus, since choosing your wine can often cause a day of stress in itself. Donald Hackett, a manager and wine buyer for Sherlock's Wine Merchant in Atlanta as well as a close friend, has provided wine selections and written commentaries that will enable everyone to feel comfortable in the vast world of wines. Look for my timelines to give you exact schedules of when to cook and even clean up. It is early planning that results in a stress-free party.

Due to the surge in demand for lighter foods and diets, I've included light alternatives for ingredients when it's appropriate. Some recipes are not compromised by the use of lighter ingredients, while others need the higher fat content to produce a good product. However, since these are "special occasion" dishes anyway, you might just decide to go all out and then make a deal with yourself to spend an extra hour at the gym.

I hope this book lights your fire to entertain and boosts your confidence in the kitchen. If you've never managed to write down all those family recipes, I aim for this collection to remind you of days gone by. Anyone can be a wonderful host with a few good recipes and a relaxing presence. Your guests are your first priority, so give them what they want: excellent food and a little quality time to spend with you.

REBECCA LANG'S
SOUTHERN ENTERTAINING
for a New Generation

Entertaining Made Easy

Entertaining on a Budget

One of the elements of entertaining as a young Southerner is usually doing so on a small budget. It's certainly easy to entertain with a small amount of money; it just takes a little more creativity.

Handwritten invitations are much more personal and cheaper than buying preprinted paper. Use paper that suits the theme, such as the colors of your favorite school for tailgating.

I'm not a big fan of e-invitations (invitations sent via e-mail) but it is certainly a way of spending nothing or next to nothing on invitations.

Making your own centerpieces and placecards using plants and flowers from your yard or patio saves expense at the flower shop. It also impresses guests to learn that you are a cook and a gardener.

Don't serve wine or liquor. Or choose to serve drinks, such as Mimosas, that are alcoholic but use a less expensive mixer.

Entertain in the afternoon when the food that is served is generally lighter and costs less to buy. Entertaining around mealtimes is always more expensive.

Eliminate the need to buy new CDs for the party music. Use your computer to access an Internet radio station. There are hundreds of stations that play every type of music to set the mood for your party.

Flow of the Party

Planning the flow of the party is essential to successful entertaining. Plan through which door guests will enter, where you will greet them, and where they can start to enjoy the food and drinks. I like to place the beverage station near where guests enter, since that's usually the first thing they want. Serve food in an area that allows guests to move to another room or area to eat after helping themselves. You don't want to have a backup in a hallway or a line for food. Of course the larger the area, the easier this is. We have a small house, and I assure you it can still be done. Open a back door onto the porch or patio if things start to become congested. Your guests should be able to move about the house freely without feeling cramped.

How Many Guests Are Too Many?

Once you start making your guest list, it's easy to invite too many people because you want to include everyone you know and love. Try to narrow down this list to create a more comfortable setting. Ask yourself a few questions to help you set an appropriate number to invite.

- *How many cars can park at your location?* Guests should be able to park and easily walk to the entrance of the party. Don't plan for your guests to have to walk down a busy street to arrive.

- *How large is your location?* Think realistically about how many people will fit in your space. An average house of two thousand square feet can accommodate about thirty people comfortably. Of course, an outdoor party can have more guests than one inside a small house. At larger parties, people tend to move around much more, so ample space should be available.

- *How many people can you seat?* Even if your party is a buffet style of service, people want to sit and eat. Don't invite twenty people if you have only four or five chairs. You don't need a seat for everyone, but you should try to make your guests as comfortable as possible. Also, if you have elderly guests attending, there should always be a seat for them.

Location, Location, Location

The location of a party is the first indication of the mood of the gathering. Always keep location in mind when choosing a theme or time of day. A lighthearted party is perfect for a back-porch gathering, while a formal cocktail party is more suited to the dining room. The location should enhance the food and mood, not hinder your guests' experience.

If having an outdoor get-together, remember to let guests know this on the invitation. The location will be a major deciding factor when choosing their attire for the party. Although it sounds like a grand Southern affair, don't attempt to have a middle of the day, outdoor, formal party in the summer. Between the mosquitoes and the heat, your guests will be more than slightly uncomfortable. When choosing a location, always think about the weather, the practicality, and the mood.

RSVP?

Invite more people than you actually want to attend. On average, about one-third of invitees won't attend. To have the size crowd that you want, invite more than you need. It's your choice to include an RSVP or "regrets only" on the invitation. The last time I tried this, very few people contacted me and I had a much larger crowd than I expected. Guests should always be courteous enough to RSVP if needed, but unfortunately they're not always this way. You know your guests—if they'll confirm with you, include it on the invitation.

The higher the budget for the party, the more likely it is that you need to include an RSVP on the invitation. It's certainly not productive to waste money on guests who aren't attending. If you are listing a contact for the RSVP, list a phone number and an e-mail address. It's much easier for some guests to e-mail than call, hence increasing your rate of confirmations.

Setting the Table Like a Pro

Setting the table can be challenging when you're new to entertaining. And it only gets more confusing when you have several courses and beverages.

However, there are really just a few rules that you have to remember when preparing the table.

Place the silverware so that the utensil used for the first course is on the outside and successive courses move inward toward the plate. When eating, start your silverware choices from the outside and work your way in. Dessert silverware is set above the plate. Forks are on the left side of the plate. (I remember this by the word "fork" having four letters, just like the word "left.") Knives and spoons are on the right side of the plate. (And "knife" and "spoon" have five letters, like "right." So handy.) Lay knives so that the blades face toward the plate.

The salad plate is on the left as well as the bread and butter plate, which is on the left above the forks. If no salad is being served, the bread and butter plate is beside the forks. Glasses should be placed on the right side above the knife. The water glass should be the first glass on the left and the wine glass should be to its right.

Seating a Successful Table

Using place cards for a party can be very helpful to the guests when locating a seat, but takes quite a bit of thought for the hostess or host. Set aside some time for planning the seating arrangement. You know your guests' interests and careers, and it's time to use this knowledge to make the gathering even more enjoyable. Sit guests next to each other who you know will have something in common to discuss. If you have two friends who love to cook, they'll be a perfect seating pair. Remember to follow a common thread around areas of the table so that, for example, one end of the table is sure to be able to discuss their interests in politics or government.

Think of guests' interest when choosing the guest list as well. It's nice to give friends an outlet to meet people they probably wouldn't meet otherwise. On the other hand, you don't want to invite people for an intimate dinner around the table if you know they won't get along.

Contrary to belief, couples do not have to sit with each other. I like to sit them across the table from each other to stimulate conversation with others. However, I usually don't sit them far apart from each other.

A good guest should be in conversation with other guests seated beside him/her. Unfortunately, this doesn't always happen. No one should ever feel left out or unwanted at a dinner party. As the host or hostess, be on the alert for a guest who may appear left out of conversation. Seek him or her out and start a discussion immediately, and attempt to involve other guests in the conversation.

Extras and Essentials

China or Paper?

Choosing the appropriate dishes for a party can be quite a dilemma for young adults just starting out. What if you want to have a formal party but you own only three place settings of china? What if you want to serve wine but only have one wine glass? There are ways to work around these issues without breaking your budget.

First of all, look at how formal your party is. If you're hosting an outdoor event on the porch, feel free to use fun, colorful paper products. A casual party indoors can also be an acceptable occasion for paper. I love going to paper stores and finding napkins and plates that are bright and airy. You can find great deals on paper products at the end of each season. For a personal touch, ask your paper store to monogram your paper napkins. Avoid the white paper plates and plastic plates from the grocery store if at all possible. If you're using paper, make it nice paper.

If glass plates are a must, first make an inventory of what you have. It's become very stylish to mix and match patterns, so don't let the fact that you have just four plates of one pattern stop you. I don't recommend mixing and matching casual dinnerware with china. Try to keep your selection in the same formality range. Silverware is exactly the same. I love mixing and matching patterns. Just don't mix silver with stainless steel.

Don't be ashamed to ask your friends to borrow a few plates or spoons for a party. Sometimes it's the best way to showcase the prettiest things. My sister and I often swap our serving items for parties. It saves us from having to buy new things.

Glasses can be a problem for most of us. We once hosted a party for forty and I owned only eight wine glasses. Thanks to my local party rental, my problem was solved instantly. I rented forty glasses for next to nothing and even returned them unwashed. Most rental businesses don't want the dishes or glassware washed so they can sanitize them. It's a perfect combo. You get what you need and don't have to wash extra dishes! Any party rental place will have plates, glasses, and silverware. Take advantage of it.

I recently picked up twelve wine glasses on sale for $2 each. Now, I'm a little more prepared for the next party at very little cost. Always be on the lookout for entertaining needs on sale.

Centerpieces for the Table

Centerpieces should be chosen by the style of dining. A buffet table can handle a large, prominent centerpiece, such as long-stemmed flowers. A table for a plated dinner should have several smaller centerpieces that allow guests to see over them. Also, whimsical centerpieces are for casual parties, while serious arrangements are for more formal entertaining.

For a sit-down dinner, I suggest buying several inexpensive bud vases and placing one or two flowers in each one. The guests can still see one another and admire the creative table. I also like to place tea candles or votives around the bud vases. Ribbons also make an interesting addition to the table.

A buffet table is a great excuse to clip some dogwood branches or large azalea blossoms and display them in a large vase or pretty pitcher. Sunflowers also make a stunning arrangement. Don't spend too much on flowers at the store before checking in your yard for "finds." Flowers and greenery from your own yard tend to mean a lot more to everyone. Whatever your centerpiece of choice may be, carry that flower or greenery throughout your home by placing a few flowers in the bathroom and other visible areas.

If flowers don't appeal, go for beautiful baked bread or fruit and vegetables. Stop by your local bakery late in the afternoon and purchase the day-old bread for half off. Pile the bread on burlap or pretty paper in the center of the table. Using fresh fruit and vegetables that fit the menu is also a wonderful way to incorporate the centerpiece into the meal. It's also a guarantee that you'll have fresh produce around for a few days.

Party Favors

While it's not essential to give parting guests a favor to remember the day, it's a finishing touch that's always greatly appreciated. A party favor doesn't have to be an elaborate gift or expensive token, just a personal item that conveys your thanks to your guests. I promise that your guests will be delighted to leave your home with such a treat.

The favor should reflect the theme of the party, just like everything else. For example, give guests a magnolia flower or dogwood blossom for coming to "A Crowd for Sunday Dinner." For a Mexican-themed party, send guests home with a fresh avocado; with a ribbon attach directions on rooting the pit for growing a tree.

If your budget is higher than mine usually is, feel free to give a split bottle of the wine you served that evening. A place card holder is also a wonderful way to work in a favor that also serves a purpose on the table. Make place cards out of small picture frames for the guests to take home.

Wrap up cookies in cellophane bags or fill paper bags with fresh cherries and a cherry pitter in the summer. I love to give out a favorite recipe that I had at the party for guests to make at home. Just print out the recipe on pretty cards before everyone arrives. If you like to use scented candles throughout your home, give guests a votive to light at home.

If you're serving Citrus Delight Ice Cream, fill bags with pretty lemons or limes. Tom's Caramel Cake is a great excuse to give everyone caramel candies for the road. Just be creative and use your personality to choose the perfect favor for all your entertaining needs.

Basic Styles of Serving

Family Style

Family style has always been my preference for family events and less formal occasions. I love to sit around a table that is filled with the food I'm about to enjoy. It not only creates conversation, but also encourages a more intimate setting.

To serve family style, simply set all the serving dishes in the center of the table and let guests pass them to each other. Make sure each recipe is in its own dish and that each dish has a serving piece in it. Once a guest is given the dish to help him/herself, they certainly need easy access to a serving piece. Also, for obvious reasons, try not to use your heaviest serving dishes.

If children are present, they should be seated beside a parent or guardian. A child is usually not able to receive a serving dish and help themselves, so there needs to be an adult nearby to assist them.

Plated Service

Plated dinners are for much more formal events and in many ways are easier to prepare. This method of serving eliminates the need for serving dishes and pieces, and therefore leaves less to wash. Serve the guests once they have been seated to ensure the food is still hot and appetizing. The table should be completely set except for the plates. Place the breadbasket on the table before dinner.

Arrange the food on the plate to look as pretty as possible. Traditionally, the plates are served to the guests in a position that places the entrée at the 6:00 position.

Remember to serve yourself last. The host and hostess should always be served after everyone else. If there is a guest of honor, that person should be served first. Serve from the left side of the guests and clear the plates from the right. Never clear the table until all guests have finished the course.

Buffet-Style Service

When entertaining for a large crowd, buffet service is often an easy option. It's a little harder to judge how much food will be eaten than with the plated service. One guest may love a particular dish and eat three helpings where another may not have any at all. The key to serving a buffet is the arrangement of all the serving pieces. The buffet line should flow smoothly without making guests carry too many items at one time.

Place the stack of plates at the point in the table where you want everyone to begin the line. I like to arrange the food in an order similar to the order of courses. I place the salad first, the entrée second, side dishes next and then the bread. When arranging the serving dishes, leave several inches between each dish to give guests room to navigate without bumping into one another. Remember to place all the appropriate serving pieces in the serving dishes.

The napkins and silverware are always last. If a guest has to carry their plate, a napkin, silverware, and a glass, it may be uncomfortable. If at all possible, serve the beverages on a different table or on one end of the table. Guests can then come back for a beverage and avoid carrying everything at once. You can place dessert on the buffet after dinner or arrange on a separate table as well. The dessert course needs clean plates and silverware. Guests shouldn't eat more than one course on one plate.

Entertaining for a Good Cause

Parties can be more than just fun; they can become great opportunities to give back to your community. Those of us who have the funds and time to entertain can put both of those luxuries to use. Asking your guests to each bring an item to donate to a local shelter or children's home is an easy way to contribute to a good cause. Simply ask the guests to bring a donation to the party on the invitation. Be specific on what you need donated to avoid confusion. After the party is over, take them to the specific charity for donation.

Battered women's shelters are often in need of kitchen utensils. Asking guests to bring a cooking gadget to a dinner party is a perfect fit. Nursing homes love to receive magazines for their residents. Encourage everyone to bring their favorite food magazine for the elderly to enjoy. If hosting "Tailgating at Home," get guests to bring a new piece of sports equipment for donating to an afterschool program.

Wine Basics

Buying Wine

The easiest way to select wine is to follow the wine suggestions listed for the menus in this book. If you are shopping for another occasion or just for fun, don't be afraid to ask a wine salesperson. You can usually count on wine shops having more educated employees than grocery stores, and they should be able to lead you to exactly what you are looking for. One place to start is just to tell them wines you've liked in the past or some characteristics you want in a wine.

Matching Food and Wine

Serving the right wine with your meal can dramatically enhance the flavor of the food. On the other hand, the wrong choice can be less than complimentary to your cooking. Remember to choose wines that are similar to the food you are serving. A wine should be as full bodied as the food it's paired with. Again, we've done the pairing work for you in the pages ahead, but try some on your own. It's a great way to learn. Just remember that in the end it's most important to drink what you like.

Storing Wine

If you're like me, you don't have a large wine rack, much less a cooler or cellar. There are several places that are not good storage places for wine, but unfortunately they seem to be the easiest places to keep the bottles. On top of the refrigerator is one of the worst places to store wine. First of all, it's warm at all times because of the heat put out by the refrigerator. Also, when the compressor turns on and off the fridge tends to vibrate—also not good for wine. Placing wine on the refrigerator should definitely be avoided.

Another popular storage area is on or near the washer and dryer. As a storage place for wine it's even worse than the refrigerator. Vibrations from the appliances stir up sediment in the wine. And besides, the laundry room (or closet) is usually one of the warmest areas in the house.

The ideal storage temperature for wine is between 55° and 60° in a dark place. For those of us without a wine cellar, room temperature (68° to 70°) will suffice for storing wine for one to two years. Find a cool, dry, dark place, perhaps a closet or pantry near the kitchen, to keep your wine. If a closet isn't available, just store the wine as far away from direct sunlight as possible. Keep the bottles lying down to prevent the cork from drying out.

Opening the Wine

Many winemakers are moving to synthetic corks and a few to screw caps. However, natural corks are still very prevalent and will probably always be. Don't let this beginning stage of enjoying a bottle of wine be intimidating. After popping a few corks you'll be a pro.

There are several glorious contraptions on the market to make this task easier. A waiter's corkscrew or the butterfly models are inexpensive, easy to use, and small enough to take along when traveling. Some corkscrews rely on the user to exert all the effort for removal, while others do all the work for you. The latter is my obvious choice. Ask the wine steward at a favorite restaurant or an employee at a wine shop what corkscrew they recommend. They open bottles every day, so they ought to know.

Serving the Wine

As a general rule, white wines should be served between 45° and 55°. Red wines are best served between 60° and 70°. If you are buying wines at the last minute, your wine shop can usually "quick chill" a bottle in a matter of minutes. To accomplish the same feat at home, simply fill an ice bucket halfway with ice and enough water to cover the ice. Place the wine bottle in the ice water and let it sit, turning occasionally, for ten minutes or until it's cooled to desired temperature.

A general-use wine glass holds 8 to 10 ounces of wine. Fill the glass only one-third full. There should be significant room remaining for swirling the wine.

Saving Leftover Wine

I used to think that wine could not be saved, so I was always tempted to "drink it to save it." You may like this method, but there are other options. The key to saving leftover wine is to eliminate its exposure to air. Tightly replace the cork and refrigerate the wine for up to four days. If using this method, allow red wine to come almost to room temperature before drinking.

There are products available that extend the life of leftover wines by a few days through processes that remove the oxygen in the bottle. Look for vacuum-type pumps that remove oxygen manually and gas bottles that displace the oxygen. Both are excellent choices for saving that bottle just a little longer. Of course, if you are enjoying the bottle with a large group of friends, as I hope you will do after reading this book, you probably won't have a drop left!

How to Be a Great Guest

- Always RSVP and abide by what you confirmed.
- Don't bring extra guests with you without confirming with the host/hostess.
- Even if you're not hungry, try a sampling of food. The host/hostess didn't cook for you to just look at the food.
- Thank your host/hostess for inviting you before leaving.
- Bring a small hostess gift. I like to take something that can be used after the party. A few examples are: linen tea towels, mulling spices, a candle, or bath salts.
- Don't leave glasses or plates in a place where they can easily be broken.
- Write a thank-you note within three days of the party if an entire meal was served.
- Don't rummage through the host's/hostess' house. Never open closets and drawers.
- If the party is a dinner party, arrive on time. You should not be more than five minutes late for a sit-down dinner party.
- If walking with your plate, hold your plate in your less dominant hand (your left hand if you're right-handed). You can usually set your glass on your plate as well and be free to shake hands.
- Go back for seconds only after everyone else has been served.
- Compliment the food, even if you don't like it.

How to Be a Great Host

- Invite a variety of interesting people. You want your guests to get to know one another, so keep this in mind when choosing them.

- When planning a menu, remember: make ahead, make ahead, make ahead.
- Relax and be comfortable. Ultimately, you will set the tone for your party.
- Give a small favor for the guests to take home. The favor can be their place-card holder or even a photo from the night. I like to download a photo taken earlier in the evening, print out a stack, and leave them for guests by the front door.
- Always have the dishwasher empty when guests arrive.
- Plan an entertaining "flow" that will ensure no backups when guests move around the area.
- Choose music to match the theme of the party. Festive background music helps even the first few guests to feel more comfortable.
- Throughout the party, pick up used cocktail napkins and dirty plates and glasses left around the entertaining area.
- Do not begin to clean up the kitchen until the last guest leaves.
- Turn on lights throughout the house. Guests tend to wander, and there should be no uninviting rooms.
- Provide directions to your home with the invitations. Make sure to include the type of dress (casual, black tie, coat required, etc.) on the invitation to avoid any confusion.
- Let guests leave at their own pace. Don't encourage guests to leave, even if it's late.
- Plan accordingly for the number of guests. This ensures there won't be a shortage of food or drink.

The Menus

Morning

Brunch for a Bunch

Miss Tom's Basic Biscuits

Charleston Shrimp and Creamy Grits

Balsamic Strawberries

Southern Mimosas

Coffee

Orange Juice

Apple Juice

Brunch for a Bunch

Brunch in the South is quite a sacred tradition. You don't have to get up so early to have breakfast and you don't have to wait all the way to lunch to eat. A Saturday morning is an ideal time to host a brunch. I find it's a great way to start off a weekend. My husband and I even chose to get married at 10:30 in the morning just so we could have brunch for the reception.

While attending culinary school in Charleston, South Carolina, I grew to love shrimp and grits. I've never tasted two recipes that were alike. Some cooks add tomatoes, some add sausage, some add wine. This is without a doubt the best I've ever tasted, and I hope you feel the same.

My grandmother's biscuits go with just about anything I can imagine. If you have time, fry some country ham and stuff the biscuits, or just smother them with Balsamic Strawberries. I have these biscuits much more often for supper, but they're the kind of food that fits any meal of the day.

TIMELINE

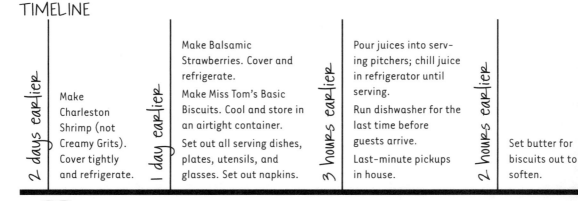

2 days earlier
Make Charleston Shrimp (not Creamy Grits). Cover tightly and refrigerate.

1 day earlier
Make Balsamic Strawberries. Cover and refrigerate.
Make Miss Tom's Basic Biscuits. Cool and store in an airtight container.
Set out all serving dishes, plates, utensils, and glasses. Set out napkins.

3 hours earlier
Pour juices into serving pitchers; chill juice in refrigerator until serving.
Run dishwasher for the last time before guests arrive.
Last-minute pickups in house.

2 hours earlier
Set butter for biscuits out to soften.

Serving Suggestions

Miss Tom's Basic Biscuits
I like to use a wooden cutting board and serve with softened butter for spreading.

Charleston Shrimp and Creamy Grits
The best way to serve this creamy entrée is in individual bowls. I prefer to pass crumbled bacon and hot sauce at the table.

Balsamic Strawberries
Serve the marinated berries in a deep-sided platter or in a large serving bowl. Remember to serve with a slotted spoon.

Southern Mimosas
Mimosas are best in a fluted glass. Use champagne flutes or wine glasses.

You'll Need . . .

Large mixing bowl
2-inch round biscuit or cookie cutter
Rimmed baking sheet
Large stockpot
Large saucepan
Large non-reactive mixing bowl

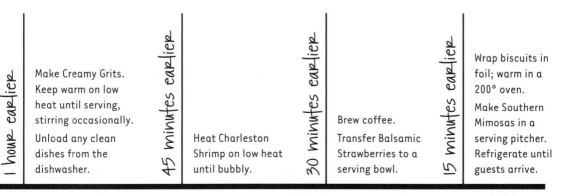

1 hour earlier
Make Creamy Grits. Keep warm on low heat until serving, stirring occasionally.
Unload any clean dishes from the dishwasher.

45 minutes earlier
Heat Charleston Shrimp on low heat until bubbly.

30 minutes earlier
Brew coffee.
Transfer Balsamic Strawberries to a serving bowl.

15 minutes earlier
Wrap biscuits in foil; warm in a 200° oven.
Make Southern Mimosas in a serving pitcher. Refrigerate until guests arrive.

Grocery List

- ○ 1 12-ounce package bacon
- ○ 1 red bell pepper
- ○ 2½ pounds fresh shrimp
- ○ 1 lemon
- ○ 1 bunch fresh thyme
- ○ 1 bunch flat-leaf parsley
- ○ 11 ounces cream cheese
- ○ 4 ounces shredded Monterey Jack cheese
- ○ 2 pints fresh strawberries
- ○ Fresh mint, optional
- ○ 2 oranges, optional
- ○ 6 cups orange juice
- ○ ½ cup apricot nectar
- ○ 1 750-milliliter bottle champagne
- ○ Buttermilk
- ○ Orange juice for drinking
- ○ Apple juice
- ○ Half and half for coffee

Check the Staples

- ○ Balsamic vinegar
- ○ Butter for biscuits
- ○ Chicken broth
- ○ Coffee
- ○ Flour (all-purpose and self-rising)
- ○ Garlic
- ○ Hot sauce
- ○ Light brown sugar
- ○ Onion (1)
- ○ Peppercorns
- ○ Quick grits
- ○ Salt
- ○ Vegetable shortening
- ○ Worcestershire sauce

Southern Entertaining for a New Generation

Miss Tom's Basic Biscuits

- Preheat the oven to 450°.
- Place 1½ cups flour in a large mixing bowl. Add the shortening and buttermilk to the flour. Stir, using a spoon, until the flour is moistened and the dough starts to come together.
- Lightly flour a surface on the counter or large cutting board. Turn out the dough onto the floured surface. Knead the dough with your hands (folding over the dough and pressing down with the heels of your palms), slowly adding more flour as needed to make a smooth dough. The dough should not be sticky.
- Lightly flour a rolling pin and roll the dough to ½-inch thickness. Using a 2-inch round biscuit or cookie cutter, cut into circles. Re-roll dough scraps, if desired.
- Place biscuits, slightly touching each other, on a rimmed baking sheet. Bake for 14 to 15 minutes, or until lightly browned.
- Serve with softened butter and jelly, or stuffed with country ham.

1½ to 2½ cups self-rising flour
¼ cup vegetable shortening
¾ cup buttermilk

MAKES 12 TO 14 BISCUITS

HOT TIP

These biscuits were my grandmother's specialty. She always used White Lily Flour because it's made from a soft winter wheat and makes better biscuits.

LIVING LIGHT

Low-fat buttermilk can be used in place of regular buttermilk.

FUN FACT

Instead of rolling out the scraps to make one last biscuit, Tom, my grandmother, folded the scraps together to create the "crazy biscuit." The crazy biscuit was usually for me.

Charleston Shrimp and Creamy Grits

1   12-ounce package bacon, chopped

1   large onion, chopped

1   medium red bell pepper, chopped

3   garlic cloves, minced

1   cup all-purpose flour

2½   pounds medium shrimp, peeled

3   cups chicken broth

1   tablespoon Worcestershire sauce

1   tablespoon lemon juice

1   tablespoon chopped fresh thyme

1   tablespoon chopped fresh parsley

    Salt and freshly ground pepper to taste

    Hot sauce to taste

For the Creamy Grits:

4   cups chicken broth

1   cup quick-cooking grits

11   ounces cream cheese

4   ounces shredded Monterey Jack cheese

- In a large stockpot cook the chopped bacon over medium heat until brown and crispy. Remove the bacon to paper towels to drain, reserving the drippings in the pan. Set the cooked bacon aside.
- Add the onion, bell pepper, and garlic to the bacon drippings and cook over medium heat until soft, about 5 minutes. Remove the onion mixture with a slotted spoon, reserving the drippings in the pan, and place in a bowl; set aside.
- Place the flour in a large zippered plastic bag. Add the peeled shrimp, seal the bag, and shake well to coat the shrimp. Using your fingers, remove the shrimp from the flour and gently shake to remove any excess flour.
- Add the shrimp to the bacon drippings; cook for 5 minutes. The shrimp will be lightly pink and not fully cooked. Remove the shrimp from the pan and set aside.
- Return the onion mixture to the pan. Add the chicken broth, Worcestershire sauce, and lemon juice. Simmer, uncovered, for 20 minutes.
- Add the reserved shrimp, thyme, and parsley. Simmer, uncovered, stirring occasionally, for 30 minutes or until the sauce is thick and bubbly. If the sauce becomes too thick, add extra chicken broth or water, 2 tablespoons at a time. Add the salt and pepper and hot sauce to taste.
- Meanwhile, make the Creamy Grits. In a large saucepan bring the chicken broth to a boil. Stir in the grits and reduce the heat to low. Cook, whisking constantly, until thickened, about 10 minutes. Then cook

for 8 to 10 more minutes, whisking often, until the grits are no longer crunchy.

- Slice the cream cheese and add to the grits. Stir until the cheese is melted and well blended. Add the Monterey Jack cheese and stir until blended.
- Sprinkle with crumbled bacon and hot sauce. Serve immediately.

MAKES 8 SERVINGS

HOT TIPS_____

Cutting bacon into small pieces before cooking saves the step of crumbling the cooked meat.

My grandmother taught me to save bacon drippings. I keep a jar of drippings in my refrigerator at all times. It adds valuable flavor to everything from salad dressings to corn bread.

This dish only gets better overnight. Feel free to make it in advance.

LIVING LIGHT_____

⅓ less fat cream cheese (Neufchatel) can be used in place of cream cheese. Low-fat Monterey Jack cheese can also be used.

Balsamic Strawberries

2 pints fresh strawberries

¼ cup tightly packed light brown sugar

⅓ cup balsamic vinegar

½ teaspoon freshly ground pepper

Fresh mint, optional

- Remove the stems and quarter the strawberries. Place the berries in a large nonreactive mixing bowl. Add the brown sugar and toss until the sugar dissolves, about 2 minutes. Add the balsamic vinegar and pepper. Stir to combine.
- Cover and chill for at least 1 hour or overnight. Stir occasionally while marinating.
- Garnish with fresh mint, if desired.
- Serve strawberries alone, over pound cake or biscuits, or with ice cream.

MAKES 8 SERVINGS

HOT TIPS

Wait to wash berries until right before using them.

Smell fresh strawberries at the store. If they don't smell sweet, don't buy them.

Southern Mimosas

- In a large pitcher or punch bowl combine the orange juice and apricot nectar.
- Add the champagne slowly just before serving. Garnish with orange slices, if desired.

MAKES 8 SERVINGS

6 cups orange juice

½ cup apricot nectar

1 750-milliliter bottle champagne

Orange slices, optional

Down-Home Breakfast

Sweet Balsamic Bacon

Scrambled Eggs with Cream

Tom's Waffles

Toasted Pecan Cinnamon Honey

Coffee

Apple Juice

Orange Juice

Down-Home Breakfast

This menu starts off the day with comfort foods everyone loves. When I was growing up, my father cooked bacon, eggs, grits, and sometimes pancakes for my mother, sister, and me every morning. We started our days at the table as a family. I guess that's why I love breakfast so much.

Tom's Waffles are another childhood favorite of mine. We try to always have some in the freezer for waffles anytime. I've added layers of flavor to bacon by coating it with brown sugar, black pepper, and balsamic vinegar, then baking it in the oven. Your guests will beg for the embarrassingly easy recipe for Scrambled Eggs with Cream.

TIMELINE

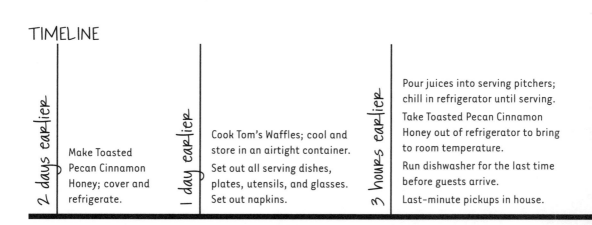

2 days earlier
Make Toasted Pecan Cinnamon Honey; cover and refrigerate.

1 day earlier
Cook Tom's Waffles; cool and store in an airtight container.
Set out all serving dishes, plates, utensils, and glasses.
Set out napkins.

3 hours earlier
Pour juices into serving pitchers; chill in refrigerator until serving.
Take Toasted Pecan Cinnamon Honey out of refrigerator to bring to room temperature.
Run dishwasher for the last time before guests arrive.
Last-minute pickups in house.

Sweet Balsamic Bacon

Stack the bacon on a small platter. Small tongs will be useful for grabbing the sugary slices.

Scrambled Eggs with Cream

A large decorative bowl or platter works beautifully for the eggs. Provide a large serving spoon for big helpings.

Tom's Waffles

Serve in stacks on a large platter. Feel free to dot with butter throughout the stack.

Toasted Pecan Cinnamon Honey

A little pitcher or a small bowl filled with honey is completed with a honey dipper or a small spoon.

Alternatively, you can individually prepare each guest's plate in the kitchen and pass the Toasted Pecan Cinnamon Honey for waffles at the table.

You'll Need . . .

Small mixing bowl

Rimmed baking sheet and cooling rack or broiler pan set

Pastry brush

2 large mixing bowls

Large nonstick skillet

Heatproof rubber spatula or wooden spoon

Medium mixing bowl

Small saucepan

Flour sifter or wire-mesh sieve

Waffle iron

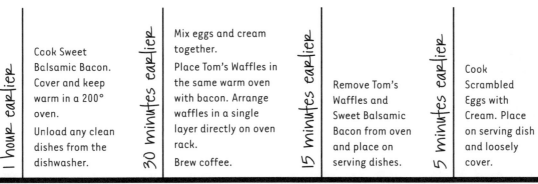

1 hour earlier

Cook Sweet Balsamic Bacon. Cover and keep warm in a 200° oven.

Unload any clean dishes from the dishwasher.

30 minutes earlier

Mix eggs and cream together.

Place Tom's Waffles in the same warm oven with bacon. Arrange waffles in a single layer directly on oven rack.

Brew coffee.

15 minutes earlier

Remove Tom's Waffles and Sweet Balsamic Bacon from oven and place on serving dishes.

5 minutes earlier

Cook Scrambled Eggs with Cream. Place on serving dish and loosely cover.

Grocery List

- 1 16-ounce package bacon
- 1 dozen large eggs
- ½ cup heavy whipping cream
- 1¾ cups milk
- 1 cup chopped pecans
- Orange juice
- Apple juice
- Half and half for coffee

Check the Staples

- All-purpose flour
- Baking powder
- Balsamic vinegar
- Butter
- Cinnamon
- Coffee
- Honey
- Light brown sugar
- Nonstick cooking spray
- Peppercorns
- Salt
- Shortening
- Sugar

Sweet Balsamic Bacon

- Preheat oven to 400°.
- In a small mixing bowl combine the brown sugar, balsamic vinegar, and pepper.
- Line a rimmed baking sheet or the bottom pan of a broiler set with aluminum foil. If using a baking sheet, place an ovenproof cooling rack over the foil. If using a broiler set, top the foil with the broiling rack. Lightly spray the rack with nonstick cooking spray. Arrange the bacon on the rack in a single layer.
- Using a pastry brush coat the bacon generously with the brown sugar mixture. Bake for 25 to 30 minutes or until the bacon is slightly crispy, or until the desired doneness is reached.

½   cup packed light brown sugar

1½ tablespoons balsamic vinegar

1   teaspoon freshly ground pepper

1   16-ounce package sliced bacon

MAKES 6 TO 8 SERVINGS

HOT TIPS

Expect a little smoke when cooking bacon in the oven. Just turn on your exhaust fan or open a window to vent.

Light brown sugar has a lighter flavor than dark brown sugar. But feel free to just use what you have on hand.

Scrambled Eggs with Cream

10 large eggs
½ cup heavy whipping cream
½ teaspoon salt
¼ teaspoon freshly ground pepper
2 tablespoons butter

- In a large mixing bowl combine the eggs and cream. Whisk until blended. Add the salt and pepper.
- In a large nonstick skillet melt the butter over medium heat. Add the eggs. Using a heatproof rubber spatula or a wooden spoon gently move the eggs from the sides to the center of the pan.
- Cook for 5 to 6 minutes, gently stirring, until the eggs are fluffy and cooked through.

MAKES 6 TO 8 SERVINGS

HOT TIP

Cracking eggs on a flat surface, like the countertop, makes a straighter break. This helps to keep little pieces of shell from ending up on your plate.

Tom's Waffles

- In a medium mixing bowl combine the flour, baking powder, salt, and sugar.
- Using an electric mixer beat the egg whites until stiff; set aside.
- In a large mixing bowl whisk the egg yolks until pale yellow; add the milk. Add the dry ingredients to the yolk mixture; stir just until combined.
- In a small saucepan over low heat melt the shortening. Add the melted shortening to the batter. Fold in the beaten egg whites.
- Using a waffle iron cook the batter according to the manufacturer's instructions.
- Serve with Toasted Pecan Cinnamon Honey or maple syrup.

1¾	cups sifted all-purpose flour
2	teaspoons baking powder
1	teaspoon salt
2	tablespoons sugar
2	large eggs, separated
1¾	cups milk
6	tablespoons shortening

MAKES 8 BELGIAN WAFFLES (OR MORE REGULAR WAFFLES)

HOT TIPS

If making waffles ahead, reheat them in the toaster. If making waffles right before serving, keep them warm by placing in a 200° oven. Set them directly on the middle oven rack in a single layer.

Waffles can be frozen for up to 2 months by placing sheets of waxed paper between waffles and sealing in a zippered plastic freezer bag.

Toasted Pecan Cinnamon Honey

1   cup chopped pecans
½   teaspoon ground cinnamon
1⅓   cups honey

- Preheat the oven to 250°.
- Place the pecans on a rimmed baking sheet. Spray the pecans lightly with nonstick cooking spray. Sprinkle evenly with cinnamon.
- Bake for 12 minutes.
- Let cool for 5 minutes.
- In a small bowl combine the cooled pecans and honey.

MAKES 2 CUPS

HOT TIPS

Toasting nuts brings out the natural oils and intensifies the flavor.

This recipe can be made ahead, covered, and stored in the refrigerator for up to 3 days. Allow to come to room temperature before serving.

Buying chopped pecans saves money over buying pecan halves.

Fruit Fantasy

Breakfast Smoothies
Very Blueberry Muffins
Banana–White Chocolate Muffins
Raspberry Butter
Peach Butter
Orange Juice
Coffee

Fruit Fantasy

Try this menu for a quick get-together with friends, maybe before heading out on a weekend trip or a spring walk. It's even easy to pack and take on the road if needed. Muffins and smoothies are delicious ways to get vitamin-packed fruit into your diet. I can't say the smoothies are all that Southern, but they sure are fun to drink.

Banana and white chocolate are two of my favorite indulgences. Now I have them both in one bite for breakfast. I like to serve the Very Blueberry Muffins with Peach Butter, and the Banana–White Chocolate Muffins with Raspberry Butter. But of course, it's a fine excuse to mix and match. Enjoy this very flexible choice for breakfast!

TIMELINE

2 days earlier

Make Peach and Raspberry Butters. Cover and refrigerate.

1 day earlier

Make Very Blueberry Muffins and Banana–White Chocolate Muffins. Cool completely and store in an airtight container.

Freeze strawberries and pineapple for smoothies.

Set out all serving dishes, plates, utensils, and glasses. Set out napkins.

3 hours earlier

Pour juice into serving pitcher; chill juice in refrigerator until serving.

Run dishwasher for the last time before guests arrive.

Chill serving glasses for Breakfast Smoothies in the freezer.

Last-minute pickups in house.

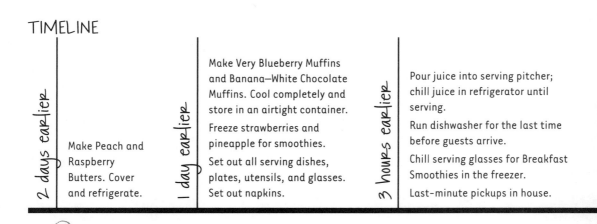

Serving Suggestions

Breakfast Smoothies

Serve in chilled stemmed glasses or rocks glasses. For extra impact, serve in the hollow body of a pineapple. If you're using fresh pineapple, this is a great way to use all parts of the fruit.

Very Blueberry Muffins and Banana–White Chocolate Muffins

Offer your muffins in baskets or large serving bowls wrapped in a linen towel or a large pretty paper napkin. They can also be served stacked high on a large platter.

Peach and Raspberry Butters

Flavored butters are great served in small bowls with spreaders. If possible, garnish the butters with a slice of fresh peach and a few raspberries so that guests will know what flavor of butter is offered.

You'll Need . . .

Pineapple corer, optional
Rimmed baking sheet
Blender
2 large mixing bowls
3 small mixing bowls
Wire-mesh sieve
2 large muffin pans
Cooling rack
Zester
Medium mixing bowl
Rubber spatula or wooden spoon
Food processor

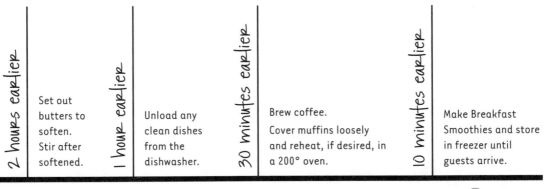

2 hours earlier
Set out butters to soften. Stir after softened.

1 hour earlier
Unload any clean dishes from the dishwasher.

30 minutes earlier
Brew coffee. Cover muffins loosely and reheat, if desired, in a 200° oven.

10 minutes earlier
Make Breakfast Smoothies and store in freezer until guests arrive.

Grocery List

- ○ 2 cups plain yogurt
- ○ 2 cups orange juice
- ○ 3 cups canned or fresh pineapple
- ○ 4 cups fresh or frozen strawberries
- ○ 1 cup milk
- ○ 2 large eggs
- ○ 3/4 cups fresh or frozen blueberries
- ○ 1 ripe banana
- ○ 4 ounces white chocolate
- ○ 1/4 cup frozen raspberries
- ○ 1 lemon
- ○ 3/4 cup frozen peaches
- ○ Half and half for coffee

Check the Staples

- ○ All-purpose flour
- ○ Baking powder
- ○ Butter
- ○ Coffee
- ○ Ground ginger
- ○ Honey
- ○ Nonstick cooking spray
- ○ Salt
- ○ Sugar
- ○ Vanilla extract
- ○ Vegetable oil

Breakfast Smoothies

- Freeze the fresh strawberries and pineapple in a single layer on a rimmed baking sheet for at least 3 hours or overnight.
- In a blender combine half of the frozen strawberries and half of the pineapple with 1 cup orange juice. Process until broken up. Add 1 cup yogurt and 2 tablespoons honey. Process until blended and thick.
- Pour into a serving pitcher.
- Repeat the process with the remaining ingredients.
- Serve immediately or freeze for up to 10 minutes before serving.

MAKES ABOUT 10 CUPS

4	cups fresh or frozen strawberries
3	cups fresh or canned pineapple
2	cups orange juice
2	cups plain yogurt
¼	cup honey

HOT TIP

Freezing the fruit for smoothies eliminates the need for ice.

Very Blueberry Muffins

1½	cups all-purpose flour
½	cup sugar
2	teaspoons baking powder
¾	teaspoon salt
¼	cup butter, melted
½	cup milk
1	large egg
½	teaspoon vanilla extract
¾	cups blueberries, fresh or frozen, not thawed

- Preheat the oven to 400°. Lightly grease the cups of a large muffin pan.
- In a large mixing bowl combine the flour, sugar, baking powder, and salt.
- In a small mixing bowl combine the melted butter, milk, egg, and vanilla extract.
- Add the butter mixture to the dry ingredients, stirring just until combined. Fold in the blueberries.
- Pour the batter into the prepared muffin pan.
- Bake at 400° for 20 minutes or until golden. Remove from the pan and cool completely on a cooling rack.

MAKES 12 MUFFINS

HOT TIP

If you use frozen blueberries, use them while still frozen. This prevents the juice from discoloring the batter.

LIVING LIGHT

1% or 2% milk can be used in place of whole milk.

Banana—White Chocolate Muffins

- Preheat the oven to 400°. Lightly grease the cups of a large muffin pan.
- In a large mixing bowl combine the flour, baking powder, salt, and sugar.
- In a medium mixing bowl whisk the egg, milk, vegetable oil, and mashed banana until combined. Slowly add the egg mixture to the dry ingredients, stirring just until combined. Stir in the white chocolate.
- Pour the batter into the prepared muffin pan.
- Bake at 400° for 24 to 26 minutes or until golden brown.
- Cool in the pan for 1 minute. Serve immediately or cool completely on a cooling rack.

MAKES 12 MUFFINS

1¾ cups all-purpose flour
2 teaspoons baking powder
½ teaspoon salt
¾ cup sugar
1 large egg, lightly beaten
½ cup milk
½ cup vegetable oil
1 very ripe banana, mashed
4 ounces white chocolate, finely chopped

HOT TIP _____

Using an over-ripe banana (one that is very dark on the outside) makes a more tender muffin and gives a sweeter flavor.

LIVING LIGHT _____

1% or 2% milk can be used in place of whole milk.

Raspberry Butter

½ cup butter, softened

¼ cup frozen raspberries, thawed

1 teaspoon lemon zest

1 tablespoon sugar

- In a small mixing bowl combine the butter, raspberries, lemon zest, and sugar.
- Strain the raspberry butter with a wire-mesh sieve to remove the raspberry seeds, if desired.
- Serve at room temperature.

MAKES ⅔ CUP

Peach Butter

- In a food processor combine the peaches and butter. Pulse until combined. Add the vanilla sugar and ginger, pulsing twice.
- Serve at room temperature.

MAKES 1 CUP

¾ cup frozen peaches, thawed

½ cup butter, softened

1 tablespoon vanilla sugar or granulated sugar

⅛ teaspoon ground ginger

HOT TIP

Vanilla sugar can be made by placing split vanilla beans in the same container with your sugar.

Sweet Sweet Breakfast

Bourbon Walnut Coffee Cake

Strawberry Stuffed French Toast

White Wine Poached Pears

Rich Hot Chocolate

Orange Juice

Apple Juice

Coffee

Sweet Sweet Breakfast

We have all woken up and craved a sweet breakfast to start our day. It not only gives us a great sugar burst first thing, but it also satisfies our sweet tooth as well. I have enjoyed French toast since I was a small child and finally figured out a way to stuff it with two of my favorite ingredients. Strawberry jam and cream cheese always make for a wonderful combination.

Bourbon Walnut Coffee Cake is for adults of course, but what a treat it is! Made easier with canned buttermilk biscuits, this homemade cake couldn't be more scrumptious. It needs to be served warm, so just out of the oven is best. Add White Wine Poached Pears for a taste of fresh fruit and Rich Hot Chocolate for yet another indulgence. After this selection, a regular sweet roll just may not satisfy you anymore.

TIMELINE

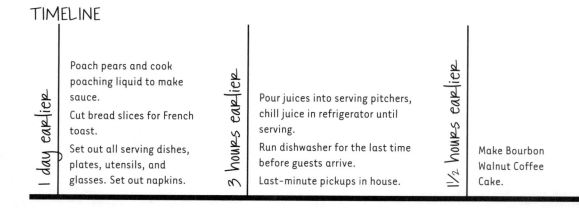

1 day earlier
Poach pears and cook poaching liquid to make sauce.
Cut bread slices for French toast.
Set out all serving dishes, plates, utensils, and glasses. Set out napkins.

3 hours earlier
Pour juices into serving pitchers, chill juice in refrigerator until serving.
Run dishwasher for the last time before guests arrive.
Last-minute pickups in house.

1½ hours earlier
Make Bourbon Walnut Coffee Cake.

Serving Suggestions

White Wine Poached Pears
Place pears on individual small plates with extra sauce. A knife and fork are useful for cutting the cooked fruit.

Strawberry Stuffed French Toast
Serve on individual plates or on a large platter. Offer a pair of serving tongs for easy pickup.

Rich Hot Chocolate
Mugs are really the perfect way to serve this frothy drink.

Bourbon Walnut Coffee Cake
A cake platter or plate really shows off my impressive but easy coffee cake.

You'll Need . . .

12-inch bundt pan
Medium bowl
Shallow bowl
Small paring knife
Large nonstick skillet
Large stockpot
Microwave

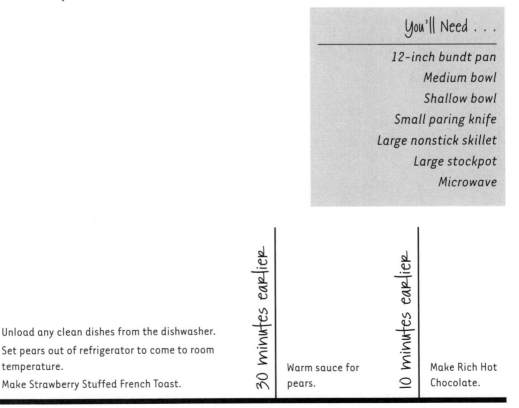

1 hour earlier
Unload any clean dishes from the dishwasher.
Set pears out of refrigerator to come to room temperature.
Make Strawberry Stuffed French Toast.

30 minutes earlier
Warm sauce for pears.

10 minutes earlier
Make Rich Hot Chocolate.

Grocery List

- ○ White wine
- ○ 8 Bosc or Bartlett pears
- ○ 1 loaf bakery bread
- ○ 8 ounces cream cheese
- ○ 8 large eggs
- ○ 3 cups milk
- ○ Hot chocolate mix
- ○ Whipped cream
- ○ French vanilla coffee creamer
- ○ Cook-and-serve vanilla pudding mix
- ○ 1 10.2-ounce can buttermilk biscuits
- ○ 1 1-pound .03-ounce can buttermilk biscuits
- ○ Orange juice
- ○ Apple juice
- ○ Half and half for coffee

Check the Staples

- ○ Bourbon
- ○ Brown sugar
- ○ Butter
- ○ Cinnamon
- ○ Coffee
- ○ Maple syrup
- ○ Nonstick cooking spray
- ○ Powdered sugar
- ○ Strawberry jam
- ○ Sugar
- ○ Vanilla extract
- ○ Walnuts

Bourbon Walnut Coffee Cake

- Preheat the oven to 350°. Generously grease a 12-inch bundt pan.
- Sprinkle the walnuts and 1 cup brown sugar in the prepared pan.
- In a medium bowl combine the brewed coffee, ¼ cup butter, and the bourbon, and pour over the pecans and brown sugar.
- In a shallow bowl combine the remaining 1½ cups brown sugar and the pudding mix.
- Separate the biscuits and cut each biscuit into 4 pieces. Dip the biscuit pieces in ½ cup melted butter and dredge in the sugar-pudding mixture. Place evenly in the pan.
- Bake at 350° for 50 minutes. Cool in the pan on a wire rack for 10 minutes. Invert onto a serving platter. Serve immediately.

½ cup coarsely chopped walnuts

2½ cups brown sugar, divided

¼ cup brewed coffee

¼ cup butter, melted

3 tablespoons bourbon (replace with brewed coffee, if desired)

¼ cup cook-and-serve vanilla pudding mix

1 10.2-ounce can and 1 1-pound .03-ounce can buttermilk biscuits

½ cup butter, melted

MAKES 10 SERVINGS

HOT TIPS

If you're not a fan of nuts, feel free to leave out the walnuts.

Do not use instant pudding mix. This recipe requires the cook-and-serve kind.

Strawberry Stuffed French Toast

8 slices (1½ inches thick) white bread

8 ounces cream cheese, softened

½ cup strawberry jam

8 large eggs

2 cups milk

1 teaspoon ground cinnamon

½ cup butter

Powdered sugar

Maple syrup, optional

- Using a small knife carefully cut a pocket in the bread slices with a 2- to 3-inch opening, leaving all sides intact. Spread 1 ounce of cream cheese in the pocket. Spread 1 tablespoon of jam on top of the cream cheese. Repeat with the remaining bread slices.
- In a large bowl whisk together the eggs and milk. Add the cinnamon.
- Dip the bread slices in the egg mixture, coating all sides.
- In a large nonstick skillet melt the butter. Cook each slice on medium-low heat for 3 minutes per side or until browned.
- Sprinkle with powdered sugar and serve with maple syrup, if desired.

MAKES 8 SERVINGS

HOT TIP

I like to cut the thick slices from a loaf of bakery bread.

White Wine Poached Pears

- In a large stockpot combine the wine, water, vanilla extract, and sugar. Simmer until the sugar has dissolved.
- Peel the pears, leaving the stems intact. Use a small paring knife to remove the cores by cutting a small cone out of the bottom of each pear. Place immediately in the poaching liquid.
- Simmer the pears, turning occasionally, until they are soft enough to easily pierce with a fork, about 40 minutes.
- Remove the pears and set aside until ready to use, or refrigerate overnight.
- Boil down the remaining liquid until it measures ½ cup. Serve the reduced poaching liquid on the plate with the pears and drizzle any remaining liquid over the pears.

2	cups sweet white wine, such as Riesling
2	cups water
2	teaspoons vanilla extract
1	cup sugar
8	Bosc pears

MAKES 8 SERVINGS

HOT TIPS

No wine around the house? Use white grape juice instead of the wine for poaching the pears.

Identify Bosc pears by their slender neck. Look for Bartlett pears if Bosc pears aren't available.

Rich Hot Chocolate

1	cup milk
3	tablespoons hot chocolate mix
1	tablespoon French vanilla coffee creamer
	Whipped cream
	Cinnamon

- Heat the milk in the microwave for 3 minutes.
- Place the hot chocolate mix in a large mug. Add the creamer.
- Stir in the hot milk.
- Top with whipped cream and a sprinkle of cinnamon. Serve immediately.

MAKES 1 SERVING

Noon

High Noon

Smashed Creamy Potatoes

Herb-Crusted Racks of Lamb

Baby Spinach with Tomatoes and Onions

Red Velvet Cake

Sweet Tea

Water with Lemon

Recommended Wines, if desired

High Noon is traditionally a time for serving the best recipes on the best china. You can do it without the china, but now you certainly have the best recipes. Here in the South, we like to eat big meals in the middle of the day. Actually, I'm not sure there's a time of day we don't like to eat big meals.

This is the time you entertain the guests you want to impress. There's nothing like seeing the looks on their faces when the racks of lamb emerge from the kitchen. With the bones crisscrossed and standing up on one another, the lamb is truly a sight to see for hungry diners. Be prepared to be slathered in *oohs* and *ahs* as the Red Velvet Cake is cut. There's no other dessert with quite the impact as this bright red layered cake. Enjoy the compliments . . . you deserve them.

TIMELINE

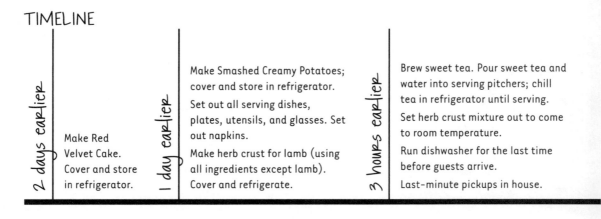

2 days earlier

Make Red Velvet Cake. Cover and store in refrigerator.

1 day earlier

Make Smashed Creamy Potatoes; cover and store in refrigerator.

Set out all serving dishes, plates, utensils, and glasses. Set out napkins.

Make herb crust for lamb (using all ingredients except lamb). Cover and refrigerate.

3 hours earlier

Brew sweet tea. Pour sweet tea and water into serving pitchers; chill tea in refrigerator until serving.

Set herb crust mixture out to come to room temperature.

Run dishwasher for the last time before guests arrive.

Last-minute pickups in house.

Smashed Creamy Potatoes
Choose your favorite large serving bowl and garnish with fresh herbs or green onions.

Baby Spinach with Tomatoes and Onions
Use a small platter or shallow bowl with serving tongs.

Herb-Crusted Rack of Lamb
Use a deep platter to serve both racks standing up with the bones criss-crossed. Carve the lamb at the table for dramatic presentation.

Red Velvet Cake
Serve the cake on a cake platter or cake plate. Be sure to cut the cake at the table. It's way too pretty to cut in the kitchen.

You'll Need . . .

Large stockpot
Potato masher
Heatproof mixing bowl
Rimmed baking sheet
Medium mixing bowl
Meat thermometer
Large skillet
Tongs
3 8-inch cake pans
Electric mixer and large mixing bowl or stand mixer
Large mixing bowl
Flour sifter or wire-mesh sieve
Cooling rack

1 hour earlier
Reheat Smashed Creamy Potatoes, stirring occasionally.
Coat lamb in herb crust.
Set Red Velvet Cake out to come to room temperature. Transfer cake to a cake platter if needed.
Unload any clean dishes from the dishwasher.

30 minutes earlier
Bake lamb.
Chop tomatoes and onions for spinach.

5 minutes earlier
Cook Baby Spinach with Tomatoes and Onions. Place on a serving dish and cover loosely.

Grocery List

- ○ 3 fresh tomatoes
- ○ 2 6-ounce packages fresh baby spinach
- ○ 2 1½-pound racks of lamb, frenched
- ○ 2 bunches fresh mint
- ○ 1 bunch fresh parsley
- ○ 1 lemon
- ○ 3 pounds Yukon Gold potatoes
- ○ 8-ounce container sour cream
- ○ 12 ounces cream cheese
- ○ ⅓ cup milk
- ○ 2 large eggs
- ○ 2 1-ounce bottles red food coloring
- ○ 1 cup buttermilk
- ○ 16-ounce box powered sugar
- ○ Fresh herbs, optional
- ○ Green onions, optional

Check the Staples

- ○ All-purpose flour
- ○ Baking soda
- ○ Butter
- ○ Cider vinegar
- ○ Cocoa powder
- ○ Garlic
- ○ Olive oil
- ○ Onion (1)
- ○ Peppercorns
- ○ Salt
- ○ Sugar
- ○ Tea bags
- ○ Vanilla extract
- ○ Vegetable oil
- ○ White vinegar

Suggested Wines

For this menu, there is one major decision to make: white or red. Both will work fine. For a white, something big and flavorful is needed because of the lamb. This is where big, rich, oaky Chardonnays work well. California and Australia lead the way in producing these kinds of wines. For something different, try a Viognier. Viognier is similar to Chardonnay in weight and texture, but expresses aromas of peaches and apricots and has a faintly fruity taste.

For red wine, use something rich but not too bold. Try a Red Zinfandel from California or a Malbec from Argentina. Wines from the Rhone region in France make an excellent choice. Because styles can vary, try to find something that has a good bit of Grenache in the blend, like a Sablet or a Cote du Rhone-Villages. Australia also produces some incredibly delicious wines made from Grenache. —D.H.

Smashed Creamy Potatoes

- In a large stockpot cover the potatoes with water. Bring the water to a boil; boil for 20 minutes. Drain and return the potatoes to the stockpot.
- Using a potato masher mash the potatoes until just a few chunks of potato remain. Stir in the sour cream, cream cheese, milk, salt, and pepper.
- Garnish with fresh herbs and green onions, if desired.
- *Note:* To reheat, place the potatoes in a heatproof mixing bowl placed over a pan of simmering water. Stir occasionally.

MAKES 8 SERVINGS

3   pounds Yukon Gold potatoes, cut into 2-inch pieces

1   8-ounce container sour cream

4   ounces cream cheese, softened

⅓   cup milk

1   teaspoon salt

¼   teaspoon freshly ground pepper

    Fresh herbs, optional

    Green onions, optional

HOT TIPS

Yukon Gold potatoes are the best for mashing. They have a wonderful buttery flavor and creamy texture.

For true indulgence, add a few drops of white truffle oil to the potatoes before serving.

LIVING LIGHT

Low-fat sour cream, ⅓ less fat cream cheese (Neufchatel), and 1% milk can be used in place of higher-fat ingredients.

Herb-Crusted Racks of Lamb

2	1½-pound racks of lamb, frenched
2	cups fresh mint leaves
1	cup fresh parsley leaves
2	garlic cloves, minced
½	teaspoon salt
½	teaspoon freshly ground pepper
1	teaspoon lemon zest
⅓	cup olive oil

- Preheat the oven to 425°. Line a rimmed baking sheet with aluminum foil.
- Place the lamb racks on the prepared pan. The lamb should be lying down with the bones curving toward the pan.
- Finely chop the mint and parsley leaves. Place the chopped leaves in a medium mixing bowl. Add the garlic, salt, pepper, and lemon zest. Stir in the olive oil.
- Using half of the herb mixture for each rack of lamb, spread the mixture on the meat portion of the top side of the lamb. Pat the herb mixture to coat the entire top side.
- Bake at 425° for 30 minutes or until the meat thermometer registers 140° (medium rare) or the desired degree of doneness. After removing the lamb from the oven, wait 10 minutes before carving.
- To carve, slice between each bone.

MAKES 8 SERVINGS

HOT TIPS

Allowing the meat to rest for 10 minutes after cooking creates a juicier piece of meat. The temperature also rises during this time, so take your meat out of the oven slightly before you want it done.

Wrap each exposed bone of the rack of lamb in aluminum foil to prevent the bones from burning and scorching.

Frenching means cleaning the bones of any meat and fat. Your butcher can do this for you.

Southern Entertaining for a New Generation

Baby Spinach with Tomatoes and Onions

- In a large skillet heat the olive oil over medium heat. Add the onion and garlic and sauté for 3 minutes or until the onions are translucent.
- Add the tomatoes and juice to the skillet, then sauté for 2 minutes. Add the salt and pepper.
- Place the spinach in the skillet (it will be overfilled at first, but will wilt down quickly). Toss gently with tongs until the spinach is wilted.
- Sprinkle the cider vinegar over the spinach. Serve immediately.

MAKES 6 TO 8 SERVINGS

3   tablespoons olive oil
1   onion, diced
2   garlic cloves, minced
2   cups chopped fresh tomatoes and juice
1   teaspoon salt
½   teaspoon freshly ground pepper
2   6-ounce packages fresh baby spinach
1   tablespoon cider vinegar

Red Velvet Cake

1½ cups sugar

2 cups vegetable oil

2 large eggs

1 teaspoon white vinegar

2 1-ounce bottles red food coloring

2½ cups all-purpose flour

1 teaspoon baking soda

1 teaspoon salt

1½ tablespoons cocoa powder

1 cup buttermilk

2 teaspoons vanilla extract, separated

½ cup butter, softened

1 8-ounce package cream cheese, softened

1 16-ounce box powdered sugar, sifted

- Preheat the oven to 350°. Grease and flour 3 8-inch round cake pans.
- Using an electric mixer mix the sugar and oil until blended. Add the eggs one at a time, mixing well. Add the vinegar and food coloring, mixing until the coloring is evenly distributed.
- In a large bowl sift the flour, baking soda, salt, and cocoa together. Add the flour mixture alternately with the buttermilk to the batter, beginning and ending with the flour mixture.
- Stir in 1 teaspoon vanilla extract. Pour the batter evenly into the prepared pans.
- Bake at 350° for 26 to 28 minutes or until a wooden pick inserted in the cakes comes out clean.
- Cool in the pans for 5 minutes. Remove from the pans and cool completely on cooling racks.
- For the frosting, beat the butter and cream cheese until blended and fluffy. Add the remaining 1 teaspoon vanilla extract. Gradually add the powdered sugar. Beat just until blended.
- Spread the frosting evenly between the layers and on top of the cake.
- Store the frosted cake in the refrigerator.

MAKES 10 TO 12 SERVINGS

HOT TIPS

To prevent crumbs in the frosting, spread a very thin layer of frosting over the cake first. This thin layer holds down any loose crumbs.

Feel free to double the amount of frosting. More frosting can never hurt!

A Crowd for Sunday Dinner

Sa's Macaroni and Cheese

Mom's Squash Casserole

Fried Chicken

Green Beans with Lemon

Apricot Puffs

Sliced Ripe Tomatoes, if available

Sweet Tea

Water with Lemon

Recommended Wines, if desired

A Crowd for Sunday Dinner

A big lunch in the South is something that every visitor must experience. We like to eat and visit until mid-afternoon before lazily making our way home or to the nearest sofa. I think I spent most of the Sunday afternoons during my childhood napping after lunch. It's always been a day for huge feasts in my family.

I relived a lot of special meals while writing this book, but this menu is the closest to my heart. I would give anything to have my grandmothers making their macaroni and cheese and fried chicken one more time. I'm sure many of you feel the same way about your treasured family traditions. The next best thing is for me to now cook those same recipes for my family. If the weekdays are too busy for time at the table, make time for those you love on Sundays.

TIMELINE

1 day earlier

Make Mom's Squash Casserole. Cover and refrigerate.

Set out all serving dishes, plates, utensils, and glasses. Set out napkins.

Fry Apricot Puffs. Cool and store in an airtight container at room temperature.

Make Green Beans with Lemon.

3 hours earlier

Brew sweet tea. Pour sweet tea and water into serving pitchers; chill in refrigerator until serving.

Run dishwasher for the last time before guests arrive.

Last-minute pickups in house.

2 hours earlier

Take Mom's Squash Casserole out of the refrigerator.

Assemble Sa's Macaroni and Cheese.

1¼ hours earlier

Soak chicken in salted water.

Serving Suggestions

Sunday dinner is best served family style. This is where every-one serves themselves from casserole dishes and platters right in the middle of the table. This service method can even make a table of strangers feel like family.

Mom's Squash Casserole and Sa's Macaroni and Cheese

Place the casserole dish in the center of the table with solid serving spoons.

Fried Chicken

Serve the chicken on a big platter. No tongs needed; just let the guests grab!

Green Beans with Lemon

Serve in a serving bowl with a large spoon.

Sliced Tomatoes

Any small plate will be fine for the toma-toes. Place a fork on the plate for picking up the slices.

Apricot Puffs

Serve on a small platter or plate that can be passed among guests after the main course is over.

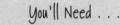

You'll Need . . .

2 8 x 8-inch baking dishes

3 large mixing bowls

Medium saucepan

Potato masher

8-inch cast iron skillet or large deep skillet

Stockpot

2 large skillets

Zester

Small saucepan

Pastry cutter or 2 knives

Pizza cutter or knife

Small mixing bowl

1 hour earlier

Unload any clean dishes from the dishwasher.

30 minutes earlier

Bake Sa's Macaroni and Cheese and Mom's Squash Casserole.

Begin frying chicken.

15 minutes earlier

Slice tomatoes, if available. Sprinkle with salt and freshly ground pepper.

Reheat Green Beans with Lemon in a large skillet on low heat.

Place trivets on the table for serving hot dishes. If trivets aren't avail-able, fold thick kitchen towels and place under hot dishes.

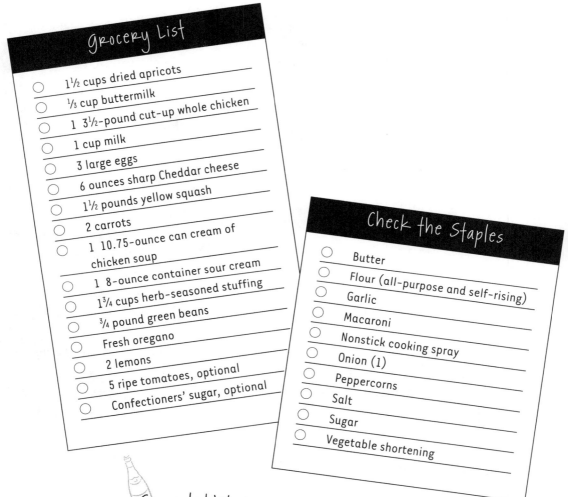

Grocery List

- 1½ cups dried apricots
- ⅓ cup buttermilk
- 1 3½-pound cut-up whole chicken
- 1 cup milk
- 3 large eggs
- 6 ounces sharp Cheddar cheese
- 1½ pounds yellow squash
- 2 carrots
- 1 10.75-ounce can cream of chicken soup
- 1 8-ounce container sour cream
- 1¾ cups herb-seasoned stuffing
- ¾ pound green beans
- Fresh oregano
- 2 lemons
- 5 ripe tomatoes, optional
- Confectioners' sugar, optional

Check the Staples

- Butter
- Flour (all-purpose and self-rising)
- Garlic
- Macaroni
- Nonstick cooking spray
- Onion (1)
- Peppercorns
- Salt
- Sugar
- Vegetable shortening

Suggested Wines

Although a nice rich California Chardonnay would be great for this menu, I prefer to offer something a little lighter in body when serving earlier in the day. Sauvignon Blanc is ideal. Right now, California and Chile are producing very affordable, very delicious Sauvignon Blancs. Styles can range from crisp and citrusy to richer and more fruit-forward. And for the adventurous, try a French Sancerre or Pouilly Fume. These are also made from the Sauvignon Blanc grape, but exhibit drier, more minerally flavors with bright acidity and clean finishes. —D.H.

Southern Entertaining for a New Generation

Sa's Macaroni and Cheese

- Preheat the oven to 350°. Lightly grease an 8 x 8-inch baking dish.
- Cook the macaroni according to the package directions. Drain.
- In a large mixing bowl combine the milk, eggs, and salt.
- Add the drained macaroni to the milk mixture. Stir well to combine.
- Pour the macaroni mixture into the prepared baking dish. Place the Cheddar cheese slices on top of the macaroni mixture. Sprinkle with pepper.
- Bake at 350° for 25 to 30 minutes, or until bubbly and firmly set.

1½ cups uncooked macaroni

1 cup milk

3 large eggs, lightly beaten

½ teaspoon salt

6 ounces sharp Cheddar cheese, cut into 20 slices

Freshly ground pepper to taste

MAKES 6 TO 8 SERVINGS

FUN FACTS

This is my grandmother's recipe for my favorite comfort food. The macaroni is suspended in savory custard, with all the cheese covering the top.

During the days when cheese was an expensive luxury, this type of macaroni saved the Cheddar for the best place—the top.

Mom's Squash Casserole

1¾ cups herb-seasoned stuffing, divided

1½ pounds yellow squash

½ cup grated onion

½ cup grated carrot

1 10.75-ounce can cream of chicken soup, undiluted

1 8-ounce container sour cream

½ teaspoon salt

¼ teaspoon freshly ground pepper

- Preheat the oven to 350°. Lightly grease an 8 x 8-inch baking dish. Sprinkle 1 cup of stuffing into the bottom of the dish.
- Slice the squash into 2-inch pieces. In a medium saucepan cover the squash with water. Bring to a boil over medium heat and boil for 8 to 10 minutes or until the squash is very tender when tested with a fork. Drain.
- In a large mixing bowl mash the squash with a potato masher. Add the onion, carrot, cream of chicken soup, sour cream, salt, and pepper. Stir well.
- Pour the squash mixture over the stuffing in the prepared baking dish. Sprinkle the remaining stuffing over the squash.
- Bake at 350° for 30 minutes or until heated through and the stuffing is browned.

MAKES 6 TO 8 SERVINGS

HOT TIP

Grating the onion and carrot makes even these uncooked vegetables tender.

LIVING LIGHT

Low-fat sour cream can be used in place of regular sour cream.

Fried Chicken

- Place the chicken in a large mixing bowl. Sprinkle with ¼ cup salt and cover with cold water. Cover and soak the chicken for 45 minutes.
- Remove the chicken from the salt water; drain on paper towels.
- In an 8-inch cast-iron skillet or a large deep skillet heat the shortening to about 360°.
- Sprinkle the chicken with salt and pepper. Coat each piece completely with flour and gently place the chicken into the hot shortening. Fry for 10 to 12 minutes per side or until golden brown, about 25 minutes total.
- Check the temperature of the oil occasionally. If the oil is too hot, the chicken will be too brown on the outside but not fully cooked through.
- Fry the chicken in batches to prevent the skillet from becoming overcrowded.
- Drain the cooked chicken on paper towels or the more traditional folded brown paper grocery bag.

Makes 4 to 6 servings

1	3½-pound cut up whole chicken
¼	cup salt
1½	cups vegetable shortening
1	teaspoon salt
1	teaspoon freshly ground pepper
1	cup all-purpose flour

HOT TIPS

Buy a whole chicken that has already been cut up at the grocery. You get larger pieces than if you cut up your own chicken. It also saves the hassle of cutting it up yourself.

Cast-iron skillets can't be beat for frying chicken. If you ever see an old, seasoned one for sale at a flea market or yard sale, snap it up!

Green Beans with Lemon

¾ pound green beans
2 tablespoons butter
1 garlic clove, minced
2 teaspoons lemon zest
1 tablespoon chopped fresh
    oregano

- Trim the stem ends of the beans; cut the beans into 1½-inch pieces. In a large stockpot cover the beans with water.
- Bring to a boil. Reduce the heat to medium-low. Simmer for 10 to 12 minutes or until tender. Drain the beans and set aside.
- In a large skillet melt the butter over medium heat. Add the garlic and sauté for 1 minute. Add the drained beans and sauté for 1 minute. Add the lemon zest and oregano, tossing to combine. Sauté for 1 minute.

MAKES 8 SERVINGS

FUN FACT

Almost every Southern recipe for green beans is done a little differently. I like these because the lemon zest lends a crisp, clean flavor.

Apricot Puffs

- In a small saucepan combine the chopped apricots, sugar, and 5 tablespoons water. Simmer on medium-low heat for 15 minutes, stirring occasionally. Remove from the heat and allow to cool. The mixture will be sticky.
- Place the flour in a large mixing bowl. Cut in the vegetable shortening with a pastry cutter or 2 knives until the shortening forms into lumps the size of small peas.
- In a small bowl combine ¼ cup water and the buttermilk. Add the buttermilk mixture to the flour, and stir just until blended and moist.
- In a large skillet heat 1 cup vegetable shortening to 350°.
- Tear off a piece of dough about the size of a plum. Roll the dough on a lightly floured surface into a 7-inch circle.
- Spread 2 tablespoons of the apricot mixture in the middle of the dough and fold the dough into a half circle (like a small calzone). Using a pizza cutter or knife, trim off uneven edges. Seal the edges by pressing with a fork. Prick the top of the pastry with a fork 2 or 3 times to allow the steam to escape.
- Fry for 3 to 4 minutes per side or until golden brown and crispy. Allow to cool before serving.
- Sprinkle with confectioners' sugar if desired.

1½ cups finely chopped dried apricots
¼ cup sugar
5 tablespoons water
2 cups self-rising flour
¼ cup vegetable shortening
¼ cup water
⅓ cup buttermilk
1 cup vegetable shortening
Confectioners' sugar, optional

MAKES 6 SERVINGS

 FUN FACT

Most Southerners call these fried pies. Our family has always known them as puffs.

Soup, Salad, and Sandwiches

Cream of Roasted Tomato Soup

Anything Goes Cobb Salad

Pulled Chicken Salad Sandwiches

Mamie's Sugar Cookies

Fresh Bakery Bread

Sweet Tea

Water with Lemon

Recommended Wines, if desired

Soup, Salad, and Sandwiches

Have the girls over for a light lunch before a day of shopping or a summer get-together in the garden. A choice of salad or a sandwich and my delicious Cream of Roasted Tomato Soup can only be improved on by sharing them with good company. Especially during the heat of the summer, I like to host a party with a lighter menu and mostly chilled foods. These recipes fit just right with the hot Southern summers.

Visit your local bakery for some fresh bread to compliment the salads. A bowl of soup and salad just aren't complete without a good piece of fresh bread. For a finishing touch, make some herb butter for spreading on the bread.

TIMELINE

1 day earlier

Make Pulled Chicken Salad. Cover and refrigerate.

Make Cream of Roasted Tomato Soup. Cover and refrigerate.

Make dressing for Anything Goes Cobb Salad. Cover and refrigerate.

Make Mamie's Sugar Cookies. Cool and store in an airtight container.

Set out all serving dishes, plates, utensils, and glasses. Set out napkins.

3 hours earlier

Cook bacon and eggs for Anything Goes Cobb Salad.

Chop hard-boiled eggs, red onion, and tomatoes for Anything Goes Cobb Salad.

Brew sweet tea. Pour sweet tea and water into serving pitchers; chill in refrigerator until serving.

Run dishwasher for the last time before guests arrive.

Last-minute pickups in house.

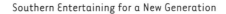

Cream of Roasted Tomato Soup
Serve Cream of Roasted Tomato Soup in a soup terrine or a large serving bowl. Soup can also be served individually in soup bowls.

Anything Goes Cobb Salad
Serve this colorful salad on individual salad plates and pass the dressing.

Pulled Chicken Salad Sandwiches
Serve Pulled Chicken Salad in a large serving bowl with a platter of sliced bread and lettuce for making sandwiches.

Mamie's Sugar Cookies
Stack these crispy cookies high on a platter or plate.

Fresh Bakery Bread
Make use of an empty basket by filling it with the fresh bread.

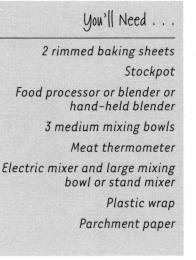

You'll Need . . .

2 rimmed baking sheets

Stockpot

Food processor or blender or hand-held blender

3 medium mixing bowls

Meat thermometer

Electric mixer and large mixing bowl or stand mixer

Plastic wrap

Parchment paper

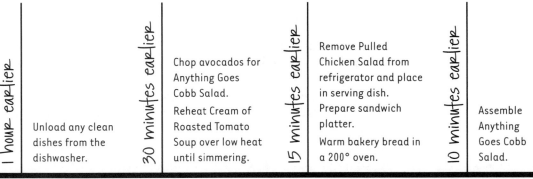

1 hour earlier
Unload any clean dishes from the dishwasher.

30 minutes earlier
Chop avocados for Anything Goes Cobb Salad.
Reheat Cream of Roasted Tomato Soup over low heat until simmering.

15 minutes earlier
Remove Pulled Chicken Salad from refrigerator and place in serving dish.
Prepare sandwich platter.
Warm bakery bread in a 200° oven.

10 minutes earlier
Assemble Anything Goes Cobb Salad.

Grocery List

- ○ 3½ pounds plum tomatoes
- ○ 3 shallots
- ○ 1 bunch celery
- ○ Fresh basil
- ○ Fresh oregano
- ○ 1½ cups heavy whipping cream
- ○ 5 large eggs
- ○ 4 boneless skinless chicken breasts
- ○ 1 bunch green onions
- ○ 2 lemons
- ○ 2 4-ounce containers blue cheese
- ○ 3 heads Romaine lettuce or 2 10-ounce bags chopped Romaine lettuce
- ○ 1 12-ounce package bacon
- ○ 2 avocados
- ○ 2 tomatoes
- ○ 4 cups of meat of choice for Anything Goes Cobb Salad
- ○ Lettuce
- ○ Sliced bread

Check the Staples

- ○ All-purpose flour
- ○ Baking soda
- ○ Butter
- ○ Chicken broth
- ○ Dijon mustard
- ○ Evaporated milk
- ○ Mayonnaise
- ○ Olive oil
- ○ Onions (2)
- ○ Peppercorns
- ○ Red onion (1)
- ○ Salt
- ○ Sugar
- ○ Tea
- ○ Vanilla extract

Suggested Wines

Because these recipes call for the use of some more forceful flavors, the wine needs to stand up to those flavors. My first choice would be to use a French Rose. Although pink in color, it is nothing like American White Zinfandel. True French Roses possess flavors of strawberries, raspberries, and cranberries. They have lively acidities and dry finishes. They are not sweet. Because they are made from grapes that usually make red wines, Roses exhibit a strong backbone without being overwhelming. Because styles vary, ask for help from your local wine steward. They may be slightly difficult to find in some areas.

If you want to stay closer to home, a lighter-style California Chardonnay would be fine. If you prefer slightly sweeter wines, try something that contains Chenin Blanc or Semillon. —D.H.

Southern Entertaining for a New Generation

Cream of Roasted Tomato Soup

- Preheat the oven to 425°. Line a rimmed baking sheet with aluminum foil.
- Halve the plum tomatoes lengthwise and place on the prepared baking sheet. Cut the shallots in half and add to the tomatoes. Sprinkle the tomatoes and shallots with salt and pepper and toss with 3 tablespoons olive oil. Roast at 425° for 45 minutes.
- In a stockpot heat the remaining 2 tablespoons olive oil and sauté the celery and onions over medium heat for 10 to 12 minutes or until tender. Add the chicken broth and simmer for 3 minutes. Add the cooked tomatoes, shallots, basil, and oregano.
- Purée the soup in batches in a food processor or blender, or using a hand-held blender, until the soup is smooth. Add the cream. Warm the soup until heated through.

MAKES ABOUT 12 CUPS

3½	pounds plum tomatoes
3	shallots
1	teaspoon salt
½	teaspoon freshly ground pepper
5	tablespoons olive oil, divided
2	celery stalks, chopped
2	small onions, chopped
2	cups chicken broth
1	tablespoon chopped fresh basil
1	teaspoon chopped fresh oregano
1	cup heavy whipping cream

HOT TIP

You can find shallots in the produce section of your grocery store near the onions. They are usually sold in plastic mesh bags in groups of 2 or 3. Shallots are known for their mild onion flavor.

LIVING LIGHT

Try leaving out the heavy whipping cream to lighten your fat intake.

Anything Goes Cobb Salad

Juice of one lemon

1 cup mayonnaise

1 5-ounce can evaporated milk

2 4-ounce containers crumbled blue cheese, divided

3 heads Romaine lettuce, chopped, or 2 heads iceberg lettuce, chopped, or 2 10-ounce bags washed and chopped lettuce

4 large eggs, hard-boiled and chopped

2 avocados, chopped

1 12-ounce package bacon, cooked and crumbled

1 large red onion, finely chopped

2 large tomatoes, chopped

4 cups fried or grilled chicken strips, cooked and peeled shrimp, or cooked steak strips

- In a medium bowl combine the lemon juice, mayonnaise, evaporated milk, and 1 container blue cheese. Cover and refrigerate until ready to use. The dressing can be made up to two days in advance.

- Divide the lettuce evenly between six dinner plates. For each plate, start with the left side of the plate and arrange the chopped eggs into a "stripe" over the lettuce. Moving toward the center of the plate, arrange the avocado (next to the egg) into a stripe. Continue making stripes with the bacon, onion, tomatoes, and remaining container of blue cheese. Top the salad with chicken, shrimp, or steak. Serve with dressing.

MAKES 6 SERVINGS

HOT TIPS

This recipe is perfect for leftover chicken or steak, or even the holiday turkey. It's also the prettiest salad you'll ever eat.

Choose an avocado that is slightly soft and dark in color. A hard avocado still needs a few days to ripen. To ripen faster, place an unripe avocado in a paper lunch bag overnight.

Pulled Chicken Salad Sandwiches

- Preheat the oven to 350°.
- Place the chicken breasts on a rimmed baking sheet. Pour the cream over the chicken. Turn the chicken to coat with cream on all sides.
- Bake at 350° for 25 minutes or until the chicken reaches 160°. Place the chicken on a plate to cool.
- Using your fingers, pull the chicken meat into strips measuring about 1 inch. In a medium mixing bowl combine the pulled chicken, celery, green onions, mayonnaise, mustard, salt, and pepper.
- Chill until just before serving.
- Serve with lettuce on sliced bread.

Makes 6 servings

4	boneless skinless chicken breasts
½	cup heavy whipping cream
⅔	cup finely chopped celery
½	cup chopped green onions
½	cup mayonnaise
1	teaspoon Dijon mustard
¼	teaspoon salt
¼	teaspoon freshly ground pepper
	Lettuce
	Sliced bread

HOT TIP

Cooking chicken in heavy whipping cream adds moisture to the meat and gives it a much better appearance when shredded.

LIVING LIGHT

Light mayonnaise can be used in place of regular mayonnaise.

Mamie's Sugar Cookies

2½ cups all-purpose flour
1   teaspoon baking soda
1   cup butter, softened
1   cup sugar
1   large egg
2   teaspoons vanilla extract

- In a medium bowl combine the flour and baking soda.
- Using an electric mixer cream the butter and sugar on low speed for 3 minutes. Add the egg; mix for 1 minute. Slowly add the flour mixture; mix just until incorporated. Add the vanilla extract.
- Place the dough on a long sheet of plastic wrap. Wrap the plastic wrap around the dough and work the dough into a 12-inch log. Wrap and chill for 1 hour.
- Preheat the oven to 325°. Line a baking sheet with parchment paper.
- Slice the log of dough into ¼-inch slices. Place the slices about 1 inch apart on the prepared baking sheet. Bake at 325° for 14 to 15 minutes.

MAKES ABOUT 3 DOZEN

Tom's Waffles and Toasted Pecan Cinnamon Honey (pages 43 and 44)

Miss Tom's Basic Biscuits (page 31)

Balsamic Strawberries (page 34)

Charleston Shrimp and Creamy Grits (pages 32–33) and Southern Mimosas (page 35)

Breakfast Smoothies (page 49)

Mamie's Sugar Cookies (page 90)

Red Velvet Cake (page 72)

Fried Chicken (page 79)

Sa's Macaroni and Cheese (page 77)

Cream of Roasted Tomato Soup (page 87)

Apricot Puffs (page 81)

Herbed Egg Salad Lettuce Rolls (page 108)

Red Potato Salad with Thyme Vinaigrette (page 165)

Tangy Pickled Shrimp (page 157)

Tomato and Kalamata Bruschetta (page 158)

Rosemary Mustard Pork Tenderloin (page 167)

Bacon Deviled Eggs (page 115)

Georgia Pimiento Cheese (page 117)

Pineapple and Orange Ambrosia (page 151)

Buttermilk Panna Cotta (page 110)

Fresh Southerner's Luncheon

Fried Green Tomatoes with
Goat Cheese and Bacon

Creamed Spinach

Cumberland Island Crab Cakes

Homemade Limeade

Very Berry Tart

Water with Lemon

Recommended Wines, if desired

Fresh Southerner's Luncheon

I was very fortunate to have grown up among an abundance of fresh ingredients. My exposure to farm-fresh ingredients is one of the pillars of my love of cooking. We all can't have green tomatoes straight off the vines or berries just hours after being picked, but we can use good-quality fresh products from the grocery.

Fresh crab meat is widely available. Cumberland Island Crab Cakes take me to my favorite place on earth without leaving my kitchen. Guests always seem to be impressed with a plate of crab cakes and fried green tomatoes. Even if your guests aren't from the South, they'll sure feel like they are by the time they leave.

TIMELINE

1 day earlier

Make Very Berry Tart.

Shape and refrigerate Cumberland Island Crab Cakes. Do not dredge in breadcrumbs.

Make Homemade Limeade. Chill until ready to serve.

Pour water into serving pitcher; chill in refrigerator until serving.

Set out all serving dishes, plates, utensils, and glasses. Set out napkins.

3 hours earlier

Run dishwasher for the last time before guests arrive.

Last-minute pickups in house.

Serving Suggestions

Fried Green Tomatoes with Goat Cheese and Bacon

Use a plate or platter for this fried Southern favorite. You can allow the tomatoes to overlap slightly.

Creamed Spinach

A large serving bowl works beautifully for this creamy side dish.

Cumberland Island Crab Cakes

Serve this seafood staple on a platter in a single layer with a serving spatula.

Homemade Limeade

Let guests pour their own sweet-tart beverage from a large pitcher.

Very Berry Tart

Don't remove the tart from the removable bottom of the tart pan and simply set it on a large flat plate. Serve the tart with a sharp knife and pie server.

You'll Need . . .

3 large skillets
Small mixing bowl
3 large mixing bowls
Medium saucepan
Electric mixer
Microwave
8-inch tart pan
Cooling rack

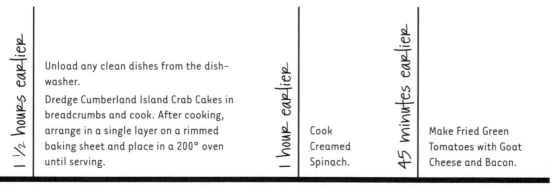

1 ½ hours earlier

Unload any clean dishes from the dishwasher.

Dredge Cumberland Island Crab Cakes in breadcrumbs and cook. After cooking, arrange in a single layer on a rimmed baking sheet and place in a 200° oven until serving.

1 hour earlier

Cook Creamed Spinach.

45 minutes earlier

Make Fried Green Tomatoes with Goat Cheese and Bacon.

Grocery List

- 1 18-ounce roll refrigerated sugar cookie dough
- 8 ounces cream cheese
- ½ cup sour cream
- 3 lemons
- Raspberries
- Blueberries
- Blackberries
- Apricot preserves
- 2 10-ounce packages frozen spinach
- ½ cup heavy whipping cream
- ½ cup shredded Parmesan cheese
- 1 jalapeño
- 1 red bell pepper
- 1 pound fresh crab meat
- Parsley
- Dill mustard
- 10 limes
- 4 large eggs
- 4 large green tomatoes
- 4 ounces goat cheese
- Milk
- Bacon

Check the Staples

- All-purpose flour
- Butter
- Cornmeal
- Diced tomatoes (2 14.5-ounce cans)
- Garlic
- Large onion (1)
- Olive oil
- Peppercorns
- Powdered sugar
- Salt
- Stale bread
- Sugar
- Vanilla extract

Suggested Wines

For this Southern meal I like a good old-fashioned California Chardonnay. Australian Chardonnay would also be a good choice. Remember not to get anything that is too oaky, as oaky wines tend to have too strong of a personality. A Fume Blanc would be a good choice, as well as a Viognier if you like wine with a touch of fruit. Although serving a red wine would not be my first choice, if you prefer reds, try a soft, fruit-driven Pinot Noir or a Grenache or, if you can find one, try a Dornfelder. Dornfelders are soft and fruity, and can be served with a slight chill. —D.H.

Fried Green Tomatoes with Goat Cheese and Bacon

- In a large skillet heat the olive oil over medium heat; add the chopped bacon. Reduce the heat to low and cook the bacon until browned and crispy. Remove the bacon from the pan, reserving the drippings in the pan. Cool. Set aside.
- In a large mixing bowl combine the cornmeal, flour, salt, and pepper. Combine eggs and milk in a small mixing bowl.
- If needed, add enough olive oil to the skillet with the reserved drippings to create a depth of ¼ inch. Heat the skillet over medium heat until the oil sizzles with a small dash of cornmeal mixture.
- Coat each tomato slice with the cornmeal mixture; dip thoroughly in the egg mixture and return to coat a second time in the cornmeal mixture.
- Fry the coated tomato slices in the hot oil for 3 to 4 minutes per side or until golden brown.
- While they're still hot, sprinkle the tomato slices evenly with goat cheese and crumbled bacon. Serve immediately.

2	tablespoons olive oil, plus more for the pan
6	ounces bacon, chopped
1	cup cornmeal
1	cup all-purpose flour
1	teaspoon salt
½	teaspoon freshly ground pepper
2	large eggs
2	tablespoons milk
4	large green tomatoes (about 2 pounds), peeled and cut into ½-inch slices
4	ounces goat cheese, crumbled

MAKES 8 SERVINGS

HOT TIPS

To prevent having "battered" fingers, use separate hands for dipping the tomato slices in the cornmeal mixture and egg mixture.

Creamed Spinach

2   10-ounce packages frozen chopped spinach

2   tablespoons butter

1   large onion, chopped

2   14.5-ounce cans diced tomatoes, drained

½   cup heavy whipping cream

½   cup shredded Parmesan cheese

½   teaspoon freshly ground pepper

- Thaw the spinach completely. Place the spinach on a stack of 5 paper towels. Pull the sides of the paper towels around the spinach and squeeze until almost no liquid remains. Set the spinach aside.

- In a medium saucepan melt the butter over medium-low heat. Add the onion and cook until tender. Stir in the drained tomatoes and reserved spinach. Cook for 3 minutes, stirring to break up the spinach.

- Add the cream, stirring constantly. Cook for 2 minutes. Add the Parmesan cheese and pepper, then cook for 2 minutes longer or until all of the cheese is melted.

MAKES 8 SERVINGS

HOT TIP

Creamed Spinach is at its creamiest when the spinach is drained of all possible liquid. Paper towels are the best way to remove all that moisture.

Cumberland Island Crab Cakes

- In a large skillet heat 1½ tablespoons butter. Add the garlic, jalapeño, and red bell pepper. Sauté until soft, about 4 minutes. Remove the skillet from the heat.
- In a large bowl combine the garlic mixture, crab meat, ½ cup breadcrumbs, parsley, mustard, lemon zest, salt, pepper, and eggs. Shape the mixture into 2-inch rounds. Cover and chill for at least 45 minutes or overnight.
- Dredge the crab cakes in the remaining 1 cup bread-crumbs.
- In a large nonstick skillet heat 2 tablespoons butter over medium heat. Add the crab cakes, and cook for 6 minutes per side, or until lightly browned. Remove from the pan, place on a platter, and cover loosely with foil. Cook the remaining crab cakes in the remaining 2 tablespoons butter.

MAKES 8 TO 10 SERVINGS

1½ tablespoons butter

1 garlic clove, minced

1 jalapeño, seeded and minced

½ red bell pepper, finely chopped

1 pound fresh crab meat, drained and picked clean of any shell

1½ cups homemade fresh breadcrumbs, divided

3 tablespoons chopped fresh parsley

1½ tablespoons dill mustard

1 teaspoon lemon zest

½ teaspoon salt

¼ teaspoon freshly ground pepper

2 large eggs, lightly beaten

¼ cup butter

HOT TIPS

Spread crab meat out into a thin layer on a rimmed baking sheet. Carefully comb through all of the meat with your fingertips to find and remove any bits of shell.

Pulse your stale leftover bread in the food processor for fresh breadcrumbs. Once crumbed, they can be frozen for up to 6 months.

Homemade Limeade

1   cup water
1¾ cups sugar
6   cups cold water
2   cups fresh lime juice
    (about 10 limes)
    Sliced limes, optional

- Place 1 cup of water in the microwave and heat for 5 minutes on high. Carefully add the sugar to the hot water and stir until completely dissolved.
- Pour the cold water into a serving pitcher. Add the lime juice and sugar mixture. Stir to combine.
- Chill until ready to serve. Serve over ice and garnish with lime slices if desired.

MAKES ABOUT 2½ QUARTS

Very Berry Tart

- Preheat the oven to 350°. Lightly grease an 8-inch tart pan.
- Press the cookie dough into the pan. Spread evenly over the bottom, and using your fingertips, work the dough ½ inch up the sides of the pan, making the sides even all the way around.
- Bake the crust at 350° for 14 to 16 minutes, or until golden brown. Cool on a wire rack.
- In a large mixing bowl beat the cream cheese, sour cream, lemon zest, and vanilla extract using an electric mixer until combined and smooth. With the mixer on low, gradually add the sifted powdered sugar. Mix until combined.
- Spread the cream cheese mixture over the tart crust.
- Starting with raspberries, make a ring around the outside of the filling. Working toward the center, continue making rings with blueberries, then blackberries. Continue until all of the filling is covered with berries. Loosely cover the tart with plastic wrap and chill for at least 4 hours.
- Before serving, heat the preserves in the microwave for 30 seconds on high, or until easily pourable. Drizzle the preserves over the berries.

MAKES 8 TO 10 SERVINGS

9	ounces refrigerated sugar cookie dough (½ of an 18-ounce roll)
8	ounces cream cheese, softened
½	cup sour cream
1	tablespoon lemon zest
½	teaspoon vanilla extract
½	cup powdered sugar, sifted
½	pint fresh raspberries
½	pint fresh blueberries
½	pint fresh blackberries
2	tablespoons apricot preserves

HOT TIP

Drizzling apricot preserves over the fresh berries adds a professional bakery glossy appearance.

Midafternoon

Afternoon Tea

Mini Cucumber Sandwiches

Herbed Egg Salad Lettuce Rolls

Key Lime Tartlets

Buttermilk Panna Cotta

*Assorted Hot Teas with
honey, cream, and sugar*

Afternoon Tea

For tea in the South, you don't have to make scones and clotted cream. We like a little more substance. Mini Cucumber Sandwiches are two mouthfuls of sheer delight. My Herbed Egg Salad is wrapped in lettuce leaves for easy pickup at the table. Thanks to past experiences, I guarantee you can't eat just one Key Lime Tartlet.

Panna Cotta is an almost sinful Italian dessert. While playing around one afternoon in the kitchen, I added some extra buttermilk to my usual recipe. Needless to say, I've never made it without it again. Once these are turned out onto your dessert plates, the guests won't remember they came just for tea.

TIMELINE

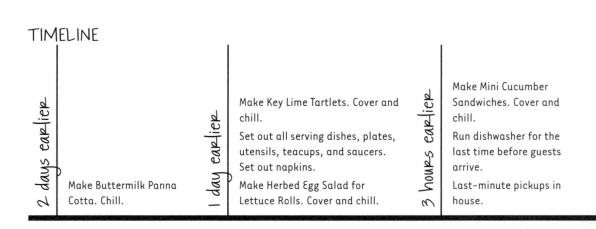

2 days earlier

Make Buttermilk Panna Cotta. Chill.

1 day earlier

Make Key Lime Tartlets. Cover and chill.

Set out all serving dishes, plates, utensils, teacups, and saucers. Set out napkins.

Make Herbed Egg Salad for Lettuce Rolls. Cover and chill.

3 hours earlier

Make Mini Cucumber Sandwiches. Cover and chill.

Run dishwasher for the last time before guests arrive.

Last-minute pickups in house.

Serving Suggestions

Mini Cucumber Sandwiches
Herbed Egg Salad Lettuce Rolls
Key Lime Tartlets
Serve all these easy to pick up foods on a tiered cake stand or on several medium-size platters.

Buttermilk Panna Cotta
Serve on small pretty dessert plates with fresh fruit on the side.

Hot Teas
There are two different ways to serve a variety of hot teas at the same time. One way is to give each guest a cup of hot water from the teapot and let them choose from a tea bag selection. If serving loose tea leaves, you will need to brew the tea in a teakettle or have enough tea balls or cup strainers for everyone.

You'll Need . . .

Medium mixing bowl
Large saucepan
Egg slicer or knife
Large nonreactive mixing bowl
2 large bowls
Small bowl
Large, heavy saucepan
Wire-mesh sieve
8 4-ounce ramekins

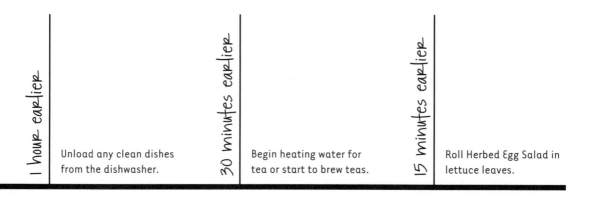

1 hour earlier
Unload any clean dishes from the dishwasher.

30 minutes earlier
Begin heating water for tea or start to brew teas.

15 minutes earlier
Roll Herbed Egg Salad in lettuce leaves.

Grocery List

- 1 8-ounce package cream cheese
- 1/4 cup sour cream
- Fresh dill
- Thinly sliced white sandwich bread
- Thinly sliced wheat sandwich bread
- 1 English cucumber or 2 cucumbers
- Bibb lettuce
- 8 large eggs
- 1/2 cup key lime juice or lime juice
- 2 2.1-ounce packages phyllo dough shells
- 2 cups heavy whipping cream
- 1 1/4 cups buttermilk
- Whipped cream, optional
- Fresh mint, optional
- Raspberries, blackberries, kiwis, optional
- Cream for tea
- Assorted teas (loose leaves or bags)

Check the Staples

- Dijon mustard
- Honey
- Italian seasoning
- Mayonnaise
- Peppercorns
- Salt
- Sugar
- Sweetened condensed milk (1 14-ounce can)
- Sweet onion (1)
- Unflavored gelatin
- Vanilla paste or extract

Mini Cucumber Sandwiches

- In a medium mixing bowl stir the cream cheese and sour cream until smooth. Add the salt, dill, and diced onion.
- Spread the cream cheese mixture evenly over the white bread slices. Top the cream cheese mixture with one slice of cucumber, then top with the wheat bread slice.
- Slice the sandwiches in half diagonally or cut with your favorite cookie or biscuit cutter.
- Store in the refrigerator in an airtight container up to 3 hours before serving.

MAKES 20 SERVINGS

1   8-ounce package cream cheese, softened

¼   cup sour cream

¼   teaspoon salt

1   teaspoon fresh chopped dill

¼   cup finely diced sweet onion

20   thinly sliced white sandwich bread slices

1   large English cucumber or 2 cucumbers, thinly sliced

20   thinly sliced wheat sandwich bread slices

HOT TIP

English cucumbers are also known as seedless cucumbers. You'll find them shrink-wrapped in most stores. Two regular cucumbers that have been seeded can be substituted.

LIVING LIGHT

⅓ less fat cream cheese (Neufchatel) can be used in place of regular cream cheese. Low-fat sour cream may also be used.

Herbed Egg Salad Lettuce Rolls

8 large eggs

½ cup mayonnaise

1 tablespoon Dijon mustard

¼ teaspoon dried Italian seasoning

⅛ teaspoon salt

⅛ teaspoon freshly ground pepper

Bibb lettuce leaves

- In a large saucepan cover the eggs with warm water. Cover and bring to a boil. Boil the eggs for 7 minutes. Peel the eggs under cool running water.
- Using an egg slicer or a knife finely chop the eggs.
- In a large nonreactive mixing bowl combine the chopped eggs, mayonnaise, mustard, Italian seasoning, salt, and pepper. Cover tightly and chill until ready to serve.
- Using small leaves of lettuce, place the desired amount of egg salad on the leaf. Roll the edges of the leaves around the salad for easy pickup.

MAKES 6 TO 8 SERVINGS

LIVING LIGHT

Low-fat mayonnaise can be used in place of regular mayonnaise.

Key Lime Tartlets

- In a large bowl whisk together the condensed milk, vanilla extract, and key lime or lime juice until blended.
- To make filling easier, leave the phyllo shells in their plastic packaging trays. Using a teaspoon, fill each shell ¾ full with the lime mixture.
- Cover and chill for 1 hour or up to 24 hours.
- Garnish the tartlets with a small dollop of whipped cream and a fresh mint leaf.

MAKES 30

1	14-ounce can sweetened condensed milk
¼	teaspoon vanilla extract
½	cup key lime juice or lime juice
2	2.1-ounce packages frozen mini phyllo dough shells
	Whipped cream, optional
	Fresh mint leaves, optional

HOT TIP

Expect to have about ¼ cup key lime filling left over. Try putting the extra filling in the freezer for a chilly snack.

Buttermilk Panna Cotta

1½ teaspoons unflavored gelatin

2 cups heavy whipping cream, divided

⅓ cup sugar

1½ teaspoons vanilla paste or extract

1¼ cups buttermilk

Fresh raspberries, blackberries, or sliced kiwis, optional

- In a small bowl combine the gelatin and ½ cup cream. Stir gently and let sit for 10 minutes. The mixture will become very gelatinous.
- In a large heavy saucepan combine the remaining 1½ cups cream, the sugar, and vanilla extract. Stirring constantly, bring to a simmer over medium-low heat. Once simmering, remove from the heat.
- Whisk the warm whipping cream mixture into the gelatin mixture. Add the buttermilk. Strain the mixture through a wire-mesh strainer to remove any lumps.
- Pour evenly into 8 4-ounce ramekins. Refrigerate uncovered at least overnight and up to 2 days.
- To serve, run a warm knife around the edge of the ramekin to loosen the panna cotta. Place a serving plate upside down on top of the ramekin and invert. Remove the empty ramekin and serve with fresh fruit if desired.

MAKES 8 SERVINGS

FUN FACTS

Panna Cotta means "cooked cream" in Italian. Once the buttermilk is added, it becomes a Southern favorite.

Allowing gelatin to sit in liquid in order to become gelatinous is called "blooming."

Vanilla paste has more flavor than extract and includes thousands of seeds from fresh vanilla beans.

Tailgating at Home

Bacon Deviled Eggs

Cool Pumpkin Squares

Georgia Pimiento Cheese

Pickled Cucumbers and Vidalias

Boiled Peanuts

Soft Drinks

Lemonade

Tailgating at Home

Even for the biggest football fan, sometimes traveling to the game just isn't possible. That's when tailgating at home is a must. To tell the truth, tailgating is the only reason I go to football games anyway! I'm much more concerned with our spread of food, or the lack thereof, than I am with the game itself. I'm just as satisfied to have our friends over to watch the game and snack at our house.

I've never seen a proper Southern tailgate without a good pimiento cheese and a spread of deviled eggs. A few bags of boiled peanuts are priceless while sitting on the couch, and Pickled Cucumbers and Vidalias have just enough dill to round out all the flavors. One good thing about tailgating at home is that you have the luxury of serving ice cream. Mix vanilla ice cream with canned pumpkin and gingersnaps, and you're certain to please your crowd of fans.

TIMELINE

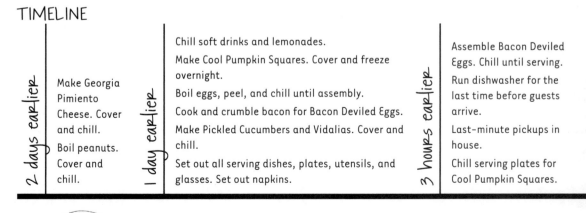

2 days earlier
Make Georgia Pimiento Cheese. Cover and chill.
Boil peanuts. Cover and chill.

1 day earlier
Chill soft drinks and lemonades.
Make Cool Pumpkin Squares. Cover and freeze overnight.
Boil eggs, peel, and chill until assembly.
Cook and crumble bacon for Bacon Deviled Eggs.
Make Pickled Cucumbers and Vidalias. Cover and chill.
Set out all serving dishes, plates, utensils, and glasses. Set out napkins.

3 hours earlier
Assemble Bacon Deviled Eggs. Chill until serving.
Run dishwasher for the last time before guests arrive.
Last-minute pickups in house.
Chill serving plates for Cool Pumpkin Squares.

Serving Suggestions

Bacon Deviled Eggs

I like these little tailgate staples on an egg platter (with indentations for the eggs to sit in), or crowd them on a small platter so they won't slip around.

Cool Pumpkin Squares

This is a great way to cool down warm Southern autumns. Place your dessert plates in the freezer and serve each square on its own chilled plate.

Georgia Pimiento Cheese

Choose your serving piece by the way you want to enjoy this dish. Feel free to use a chip-and-dip server if using the spread option. A platter or tiered cake stand is good for arranging sandwiches.

Pickled Cucumbers and Vidalias

A large serving bowl is essential for this recipe (not to mention a slotted spoon for serving).

Boiled Peanuts

Spreading out the newspaper is the only way to go. I like to stack plastic cups near the newspaper so guests can carry the peanuts around.

Beverages

Filling a metal tub or bucket is the easiest way to let guests help themselves to drinks.

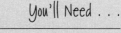

You'll Need . . .

Medium mixing bowl

2 large mixing bowls

9 x 13-inch baking pan

Food processor or blender

12-quart stockpot or 2 large saucepans

1 hour earlier

Unload any clean dishes from the dishwasher.

Let Georgia Pimiento Cheese come to room temperature.

30 minutes earlier

Lay plastic wrap on area where Boiled Peanuts will be served. Cover the plastic wrap with newspaper (preferably the sports section).

15 minutes earlier

Cut Cool Pumpkin Squares and place on chilled plates. Keep in freezer until serving.

Fill metal tub or bucket with soft drinks and lemonade. Fill with ice.

Grocery List

- ○ 1 dozen large eggs
- ○ 3 slices bacon
- ○ 1 bunch fresh parsley
- ○ 1 15-ounce can pumpkin
- ○ ½ gallon vanilla ice cream
- ○ 1 pound gingersnaps
- ○ Whipped cream, optional
- ○ 2 8-ounce blocks Cheddar cheese
- ○ 8-ounce package cream cheese
- ○ 2 4-ounce jars diced pimiento
- ○ Green olives
- ○ 1 bell pepper
- ○ 5 pounds green peanuts
- ○ 2 English cucumbers or 3 large cucumbers
- ○ 1 bunch fresh dill
- ○ Crackers or sandwich bread for pimiento cheese
- ○ Soft drinks
- ○ Lemonade

Check the Staples

- ○ Dry mustard
- ○ Ground cinnamon
- ○ Mayonnaise
- ○ Peppercorns
- ○ Pumpkin pie spice
- ○ Salt
- ○ Small onion (1)
- ○ Sugar
- ○ Sweet onion (1)
- ○ White vinegar
- ○ Worcestershire sauce

Bacon Deviled Eggs

- Remove the shells from the hard-boiled eggs. Cut the eggs in half lengthwise; remove the yolks with a small spoon.
- In a medium mixing bowl combine the yolks and mayonnaise. Stir until creamy.
- Stir in the bacon, salt, pepper, and dry mustard. Fold in the chopped parsley.
- Using a teaspoon or a small scoop spoon the yolk mixture back into the egg whites.
- Garnish with fresh parsley if desired.

MAKES 24

12 large eggs, hard-boiled
½ cup mayonnaise
3 slices bacon, cooked and crumbled
⅛ teaspoon salt
    Pinch of freshly ground pepper
⅛ teaspoon dry mustard
1 tablespoon chopped fresh parsley
    Fresh parsley, optional

Cool Pumpkin Squares

1   15-ounce can pumpkin

1   cup sugar

¾   teaspoon salt

1½   teaspoons pumpkin pie spice

½   teaspoon ground cinnamon

½   gallon vanilla ice cream, softened

1   pound gingersnaps

     Whipped cream, optional

- In a large mixing bowl combine the pumpkin, sugar, salt, pumpkin pie spice, and cinnamon. Stir in the softened ice cream.
- Line the bottom of a 9 x 13-inch pan with gingersnaps. Cover with half of the pumpkin mixture. Top with a single layer of gingersnaps. Add the remaining ice cream mixture.
- Cover and freeze for 8 hours.
- Cut into squares. Serve with a dollop of whipped cream if desired.

MAKES 12 TO 14 SERVINGS

Georgia Pimiento Cheese

- In a food processor or blender combine all of the ingredients. Process until creamy. Store in an airtight container in the refrigerator.
- Serve as a spread for crackers, on sandwiches, or as a dip for vegetable crudités.

MAKES ABOUT 5 CUPS

2   8-ounce blocks sharp Cheddar cheese, cut into 1-inch cubes

1   8-ounce package cream cheese, softened

2   4-ounce jars diced pimiento, drained

10 green olives, diced

½   red or green bell pepper, finely chopped

1   tablespoon finely chopped onion

1   cup mayonnaise

2   tablespoons Worcestershire sauce

    Freshly ground pepper to taste

HOT TIP

Chop bell peppers by slicing off the top and the bottom. Then slice down the side of the pepper to open up the "ring." Remove the seeds and membrane. You should now have a flat rectangle of pepper to chop.

LIVING LIGHT

Low-fat Cheddar cheese, ⅓ less fat cream cheese (Neufchatel), and low-fat mayonnaise can be used in place of regular cheeses and mayonnaise.

Pickled Cucumbers and Vidalias

¾ cup sugar

1 cup white vinegar

½ teaspoon salt

½ teaspoon freshly ground pepper

2 English cucumbers, thinly sliced, or 3 large cucumbers, seeded and thinly sliced

1 medium Vidalia onion or other sweet onion, halved and thinly sliced

¼ cup chopped fresh dill

- In a large mixing bowl whisk the sugar, vinegar, salt, and pepper until the sugar is dissolved. Add the cucumbers and onion. Stir well. Stir in the fresh dill.
- Cover and chill for 8 hours.
- Serve with a slotted spoon.

MAKES 8 TO 10 SERVINGS

HOT TIP

This recipe can be made right in the serving bowl to save on cleanup.

Boiled Peanuts

- Rinse the peanuts with cold water.
- Place the peanuts and salt in a 12-quart stockpot or 2 large saucepans and cover with water. Bring to a boil. Boil for 2½ hours.
- Remove from the heat and allow the peanuts to sit in the water for 30 minutes.
- Drain and serve or store in the refrigerator until ready to serve. Boiled peanuts can be reheated in the microwave if desired.

5   pounds green peanuts in shells

¾   cup salt

MAKES ABOUT 15 TO 20 SERVINGS

HOT TIPS

Green peanuts are immature peanuts. If you're not sure if the nuts are immature, break one open and look at the inside of the shell. An immature peanut's shell is white or light gray on the inside. A shell that is dark brown on the inside is mature.

You can find green peanuts at some grocery stores or farmers' markets, or surely at the best option, roadside vegetable stands.

By the time green peanuts have arrived at the stores, they've aged enough to require a longer cooking time (as in the recipe). If you're ever lucky enough to pick green peanuts in the field, they need only about 30 minutes of cooking time.

Cocktails on the Porch

Vodka Coolers

Mojitos

Mango Margaritas

Bellinis

Sweet and Spicy Peanut Brittle

Fiery Toasted Cashews

Cocktails on the Porch

Celebrate the arrival of spring by having a party outdoors. Gathering for drinks in the late afternoon gives a much-needed dose of fresh air. This is a great place to start for first-time hosts and hostesses.

These are not necessarily Southern drinks, they're just *my* favorite drinks. I hope you enjoy them as much as I do. I encourage you to have your friends over on a warm evening and enjoy these refreshing drinks and some hot and spicy snacks. I never have leftovers of my Sweet and Spicy Peanut Brittle. Eating it is quite addictive. You may find the Fiery Cashews have exactly the same effect.

TIMELINE

2 days earlier
Make Fiery Toasted Cashews. Store in an airtight container.

1 day earlier
Set out all glasses and serving dishes. Set out cocktail napkins.
Make Sweet and Spicy Peanut Brittle. Store in an airtight container.

3 hours earlier
Run dishwasher for the last time before guests arrive.
Last-minute pickups in house.

1 hour earlier
Unload any clean dishes from the dishwasher.

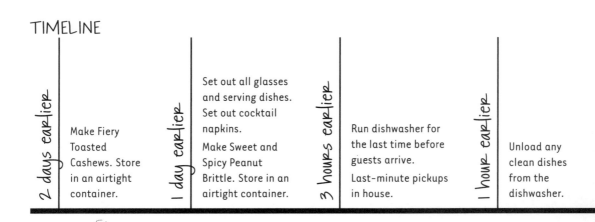

Serving Suggestions

Vodka Coolers
Serve Vodka Coolers in rocks glasses or vodka shooter glasses (if you're lucky enough to own them).

Mojitos
Serve Mojitos in highball glasses.

Mango Margaritas
Pull out those margarita glasses. These frosty drinks are best in stemmed glasses.

Bellinis
Champagne flutes are perfect for Bellinis.

Sweet and Spicy Peanut Brittle
Serve small amounts at a time on a tray or platter. The brittle gets sticky if left out too long.

Fiery Toasted Cashews
These cashews will go fast. It's better to put them in a big serving bowl.

You'll Need . . .

Shallow bowl

Pitcher

Blender

Rimmed baking sheet

Heavy saucepan

Candy thermometer

Large mixing bowl

30 minutes earlier
Make Vodka Coolers. Chill until ready to serve.

15 minutes earlier
Make Mango Margaritas. Store in the freezer until guests arrive.
Make Bellinis. Chill until guests arrive.

throughout the party
Make Mojitos as needed. They're best made individually.

Grocery List

- 2 mangoes
- 1 cup mango nectar
- 1 750-milliliter bottle champagne
- 3½ cups peach nectar
- Fresh peaches, optional
- 1 lemon
- 4 oranges
- 2 cups roasted salted peanuts
- 4 cups salted cashews
- Limes
- Fresh mint
- Club soda
- Tonic water

Check the Staples

- Baking soda
- Butter
- Cayenne pepper
- Garlic powder
- Ground cinnamon
- Light corn syrup
- Paprika
- Salt
- Soy sauce
- Sugar
- Tequila
- Triple Sec
- Vegetable oil
- Vodka
- White rum
- Worcestershire sauce

Southern Entertaining for a New Generation

Vodka Coolers

- Pour ½ cup orange juice in a shallow bowl. Pour ¼ cup sugar on a plate.
- Dip the rims of the glasses in the orange juice, then the sugar.
- In a pitcher combine the tonic water, vodka, Triple Sec, juices, and sugar. Serve over ice. Garnish with orange slices if desired.

MAKES 3 CUPS

½ cup orange juice
¼ cup sugar
16 ounces tonic water
4 ounces vodka
1 ounce Triple Sec
Juice of 1 lemon
Juice of 1 orange
1 tablespoon superfine sugar or sugar
Orange slices, optional

HOT TIP

Superfine sugar dissolves much faster than granulated sugar. You can make your own superfine sugar by pulsing granulated sugar in the food processor several times.

Mojitos

For each 8-ounce drink:

Juice of half a lime

1 tablespoon superfine sugar
or sugar

2 tablespoons fresh mint
leaves, torn

1 ounce white rum

6½ ounces club soda

Ice

- In a highball glass combine the lime juice, sugar, and mint, stirring vigorously. Add the rum and soda, and stir.
- Top with the desired amount of ice and serve with a drinking straw.

MAKES 1 SERVING

Mango Margaritas

- Cut the mango meat from the fruit and place in a blender. Add about 2 tablespoons mango nectar. Purée.
- Add the ice and blend until the ice is crushed. Add the remaining mango nectar, sugar, and tequila. Purée until blended.

MAKES 4 TO 6 SERVINGS

2   fresh mangos

1   cup mango nectar

4½ cups ice

¼   cup superfine sugar or sugar

½   to ¾ cup tequila

HOT TIPS

Choose a fresh mango that is slightly soft to the touch. To remove the meat, halve the mango and score the meat with a small paring knife in a grid formation. Then you can just press on the skin side of the mango with your fingers, turning the mango half "inside out," and the pieces will extend for easy removal.

Look for mango nectar in the juice section of the grocery store.

Bellinis

1 750-milliliter bottle champagne or sparkling wine

3½ cups peach nectar

Fresh peach slices, optional

- Combine the champagne and peach nectar. Chill until ready to serve.
- Garnish each glass with a peach slice if desired.

MAKES 7 CUPS

Sweet and Spicy Peanut Brittle

- Grease a rimmed baking sheet and a spatula with 2 tablespoons vegetable oil. Set aside.
- In a heavy saucepan combine the sugar, water, and corn syrup. Attach a candy thermometer to the saucepan. Bring the sugar mixture to a boil over medium heat. Boil until the sugar mixture reaches 340°, stirring occasionally.
- Remove the saucepan from the heat. Working quickly, stir in the baking soda, cayenne pepper, cinnamon, and peanuts. The mixture will bubble when you add the baking soda.
- Pour the peanut mixture onto the prepared baking sheet. Spread to about ¼-inch thickness with the greased spatula. The mixture will not cover the length of the pan.
- Allow to cool completely; break into pieces. Store in an airtight container.

2	tablespoons vegetable oil
2	cups sugar
½	cup water
¾	cup light corn syrup
1½	teaspoons baking soda
½	teaspoon cayenne pepper
¼	teaspoon ground cinnamon
2	cups roasted salted peanuts

MAKES ABOUT 25 SERVINGS

HOT TIPS

Soak the saucepan overnight or boil clean water in it for a few minutes to clean completely.

Peanut brittle tends to get sticky if left out. Only set out as much as you'll eat at a time.

Fiery Toasted Cashews

¼ cup butter, melted

½ teaspoon garlic powder

2 tablespoons Worcestershire sauce

¼ cup soy sauce

1 teaspoon cayenne pepper

1 teaspoon salt

½ teaspoon paprika

4 cups salted cashews

- Preheat the oven to 325°.
- In a large mixing bowl combine the melted butter, garlic powder, Worcestershire sauce, soy sauce, cayenne pepper, salt, and paprika. Add the cashews and toss well to coat.
- Spread the cashews in a single layer on a rimmed baking sheet. Bake at 325° for 20 minutes, stirring once.
- Drain and cool the cashews on several layers of paper towels.

MAKES 4 CUPS

Picnic at Dusk

Cheese Tortellini and Sun-Dried Tomato Salad

Herb-Roasted Asparagus

Spinach Salad with Toasted Pecans

Black-and-White Chocolate Mint Brownies

Bottled Water

Recommended Wines, if desired

Picnic at Dusk

Enjoying delicious food and wonderful friends at a nice afternoon picnic is a true luxury in life. Of course, the weather and the friends play a big role, but the food is always the star. This won't be the same old picnic with ham sandwiches and chips. You'll dazzle your guests even without your kitchen nearby. Pull your favorite quilt or a colorful blanket out of the closet and look for an inspiring location for the perfect picnic.

I encourage you to take time to picnic with your family and friends. It often eliminates much of the stress of entertaining in your home, but still offers the pleasure of company. You'll find this timeline and the recipes much quicker to accomplish since no home preparation is needed. Remember to have fun and discover the wonderful outdoors the South has to offer.

TIMELINE

2 days earlier

Set out all storage containers for transporting food to the picnic site.

Set out serving dishes, plates, and utensils. Set out napkins.

Chill bottled waters.

1 day earlier

Make Cheese Tortellini and Sun-Dried Tomato Salad. Cover and refrigerate.

Make Balsamic Vinaigrette. Cover and refrigerate.

Toast pecans; slice onion and tomatoes for Spinach Salad with Toasted Pecans.

Make Black-and-White Chocolate Mint Brownies.

Serving Suggestions

Place all recipes in separate plastic containers or bags for transportation. The Cheese Tortellini and Sun-Dried Tomato Salad needs to be transported in a cooler.

Cheese Tortellini and Sun-Dried Tomato Salad
A trifle dish or large serving bowl is a wonderful choice for this popular pasta salad.

Herb-Roasted Asparagus
I like to serve asparagus stacked on a small platter with tongs or a large fork.

Spinach Salad with Toasted Pecans
A small serving platter or large bowl holds the salad as well as shows off the pretty colors.

Black-and-White Chocolate Mint Brownies
A small plate or cake stand is ideal for the chocolate treats.

You'll Need . . .

Large saucepan
Colander
Large mixing bowl
Large zippered plastic bag
Rimmed baking sheet
2-cup measuring cup
9 x 9-inch pan
Cooling rack

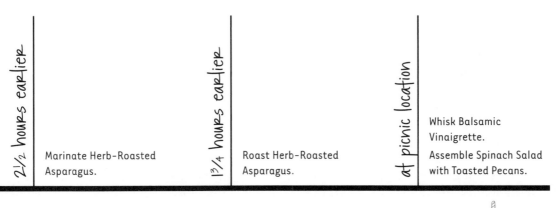

2½ hours earlier
Marinate Herb-Roasted Asparagus.

1¾ hours earlier
Roast Herb-Roasted Asparagus.

at picnic location
Whisk Balsamic Vinaigrette.
Assemble Spinach Salad with Toasted Pecans.

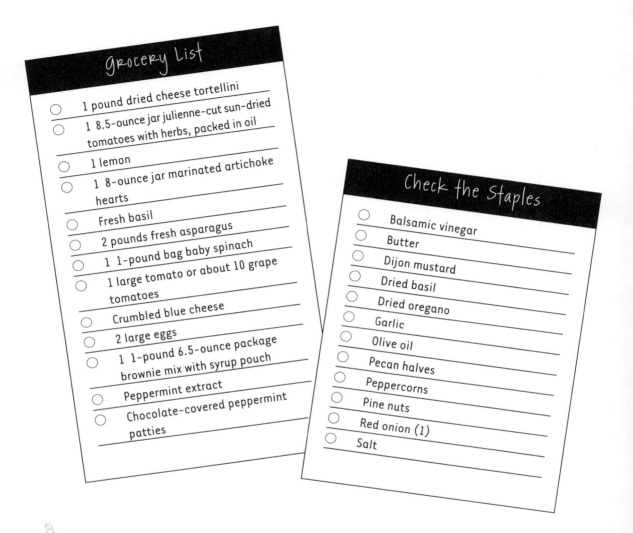

Grocery List

- 1 pound dried cheese tortellini
- 1 8.5-ounce jar julienne-cut sun-dried tomatoes with herbs, packed in oil
- 1 lemon
- 1 8-ounce jar marinated artichoke hearts
- Fresh basil
- 2 pounds fresh asparagus
- 1 1-pound bag baby spinach
- 1 large tomato or about 10 grape tomatoes
- Crumbled blue cheese
- 2 large eggs
- 1 1-pound 6.5-ounce package brownie mix with syrup pouch
- Peppermint extract
- Chocolate-covered peppermint patties

Check the Staples

- Balsamic vinegar
- Butter
- Dijon mustard
- Dried basil
- Dried oregano
- Garlic
- Olive oil
- Pecan halves
- Peppercorns
- Pine nuts
- Red onion (1)
- Salt

Suggested Wines

Because asparagus is a rather difficult food to pair with wine, the choices are somewhat reduced. I find that fruity white wines or roses work best. Try a Pinot Blanc or Gewurztraminer from either the United States or France's Alsace region. Australia and New Zealand also make some delicious Gewurztraminers. You could also try any of the fruity American blends; look for grapes like Muscat, Semillon, or Chenin Blanc blended with Sauvignon Blanc or Chardonnay. Red wine would not be a choice I would recommend, but if you insist, look for soft reds like Beaujolais, Cote du Rhone, or Pinot Noir. —D.H.

Cheese Tortellini and Sun-Dried Tomato Salad

- Cook the pasta according to the package directions. Drain and cool.
- Drain the tomatoes, reserving ⅓ cup oil from the jar.
- In a large mixing bowl combine the reserved oil, lemon juice, garlic, salt, and pepper. Whisk to combine.
- Add the tomatoes, artichoke hearts, and pine nuts to the oil mixture. Add the tortellini and toss to combine.
- Let stand for 30 minutes at room temperature if serving immediately, or cover and chill up to 2 days.
- Garnish with fresh basil before serving.

MAKES 8 SERVINGS

1 pound dried cheese tortellini

1 8.5-ounce jar julienne-cut sun-dried tomatoes with herbs, packed in oil

Juice of 1 lemon

2 cloves garlic, minced

½ teaspoon salt

1 teaspoon freshly ground pepper

1 8-ounce jar marinated artichoke hearts, drained

½ cup pine nuts, toasted

Fresh basil

HOT TIPS

Toast the pine nuts on a rimmed baking sheet in a 250° oven for 8 to 10 minutes. Watch carefully to prevent burning.

Herb-Roasted Asparagus

3 tablespoons balsamic vinegar

1 tablespoon dried basil

2 teaspoons dried oregano

1 teaspoon salt

1 teaspoon freshly ground pepper

2 pounds fresh asparagus, trimmed

- In a large zippered plastic bag combine the balsamic vinegar, basil, oregano, salt, and pepper.
- Add the trimmed asparagus; close the bag. Shake the bag to coat the asparagus. Let the asparagus marinate in the bag for 45 minutes.
- Preheat the oven to 500°.
- Remove the asparagus from the bag and arrange on a rimmed baking sheet. Pour any remaining marinade over the asparagus.
- Bake at 500° for 8 minutes, turning once. (Asparagus will be slightly charred and wilted.)

MAKES 8 SERVINGS

HOT TIP

Trimming asparagus takes off the tough ends of the stalks. Hold the bottom of the stalk and wiggle the asparagus until it snaps. This is an easy way to show the general amount that needs to be trimmed off the bottom of the stalk.

Spinach Salad with Toasted Pecans

- Arrange the spinach on a serving platter.
- Top the spinach with red onion, tomatoes, blue cheese, and pecans. Drizzle with Balsamic Vinaigrette. Toss before serving.

MAKES 6 TO 8 SERVINGS

1   1-pound bag baby spinach, washed and dried

½   red onion, thinly sliced

½   cup chopped tomatoes or halved grape tomatoes

⅓   cup crumbled blue cheese

¼   cup pecan halves, toasted

Balsamic Vinaigrette (see recipe on the next page)

HOT TIP

Read the bag of spinach before washing. Some brands come already washed and ready to be used.

Balsamic Vinaigrette

⅓ cup balsamic vinegar

1 tablespoon Dijon mustard

¼ teaspoon salt

⅛ teaspoon freshly ground pepper

⅔ cup olive oil

- In a 2-cup measuring cup combine the balsamic vinegar, mustard, salt, and pepper. Whisk to combine.
- While whisking vigorously, slowly add the olive oil.

MAKES 1 CUP

HOT TIP

Whisking while adding olive oil incorporates the oil into the vinegar. This helps to slow the separation process.

Black-and-White Chocolate Mint Brownies

- Preheat the oven to 350°. Line a 9 x 9-inch pan with aluminum foil. Lightly grease the aluminum foil or spray with nonstick cooking spray.
- In a large mixing bowl combine the brownie mix, melted butter, and water until moistened. Add the syrup pouch and eggs, stirring until incorporated. Stir in the peppermint extract.
- Cut each mint patty into 6 even pieces. Stir the pieces into the batter.
- Pour the batter into the prepared pan. Bake at 350° for 30 minutes.
- Cool completely in the pan on a cooling rack. Once cool, gently lift the foil from the pan. Cut the brownies into squares.

MAKES 16 SERVINGS

1	1-pound 6.5-ounce package brownie mix with syrup pouch
⅓	cup butter, melted
¼	cup water
2	large eggs, slightly beaten
½	teaspoon peppermint extract
10	chocolate-covered peppermint patties

HOT TIP _____

A pizza cutter makes cutting brownies and bar cookies much easier than cutting with a knife.

Evening

Seafood Supper Club

Pecan Smoked Trout Spread

Spicy Catfish Sandwiches

Old-Fashioned Potato Salad

Pineapple and Orange Ambrosia

Water with Lemon

Sweet Tea

Recommended Wines, if desired

Seafood Supper Club

Some of my college friends and a few others meet once a month for supper club. It's our way to stay in touch when we are all so busy with everyday life. We meet at a different person's house each month and catch up as if we were still in school. We choose to leave our husbands and significant others at home so we can enjoy some "girl time" to ourselves. Some members of our group are climbing the corporate ladder, some are starting families, and some of us are just trying to make a place for ourselves, but the dinner table is our way of coming together.

Whether it be new friends or longtime companions, friendships are grown and nurtured over good food. Start a supper club of your own and take some time to build your friendships. You'll be glad you did.

This menu is dedicated to my supper club:
Natalie, Ginna, Emily, Callie, Jennifer,
Leslie, Christie, Summer, and Courtney.
Thanks for your friendship and all the good food!

TIMELINE

2 days earlier

Make Zesty Mayonnaise. Cover and chill until serving.

Set out all serving dishes, plates, utensils, and glasses. Set out napkins.

1 day earlier

Make Old-Fashioned Potato Salad. Place in serving bowl, cover, and chill.

Make Pecan Smoked Trout Spread. Place in serving dish, cover, and chill.

Make Pineapple and Orange Ambrosia, cover, and chill.

3 hours earlier

Brew sweet tea. Pour tea and water into serving pitchers. Chill in refrigerator until serving.

Run dishwasher for the last time before guests arrive.

Last-minute pickups in house.

Pecan Smoked Trout Spread

A chip-and-dip bowl is just right for this delightful spread and crackers. If you don't have one of these, try a small platter for the crackers and a small serving bowl for the spread. Don't forget the spreader.

Spicy Catfish Sandwiches

A large platter filled with sandwiches is very inviting paired with a small bowl for the Zesty Mayonnaise. A tray or even a large wooden cutting board is also a good way to show off the sandwiches.

Old-Fashioned Potato Salad

A large serving bowl is ideal for potato salad. But if you don't have one, you can always mound it on a pretty plate or shallow platter.

Pineapple and Orange Ambrosia

I love to use parfait glasses, wine glasses, martini glasses, or small bowls for each guest when I'm serving ambrosia. It's an easy way to dress up your dessert.

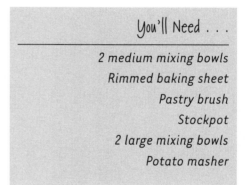

You'll Need . . .

2 medium mixing bowls
Rimmed baking sheet
Pastry brush
Stockpot
2 large mixing bowls
Potato masher

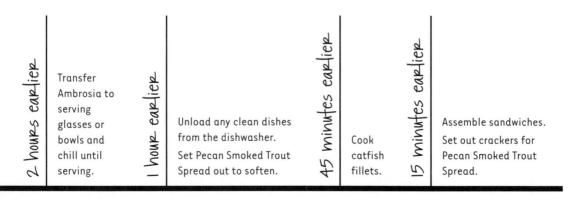

2 hours earlier

Transfer Ambrosia to serving glasses or bowls and chill until serving.

1 hour earlier

Unload any clean dishes from the dishwasher.

Set Pecan Smoked Trout Spread out to soften.

45 minutes earlier

Cook catfish fillets.

15 minutes earlier

Assemble sandwiches.

Set out crackers for Pecan Smoked Trout Spread.

Grocery List

- ½ pound pecan smoked trout
- 1 8-ounce package cream cheese
- ⅓ cup sour cream
- 1 bunch fresh dill
- 1 lemon
- 4 6-ounce catfish fillets
- 1 16-ounce loaf French bread
- 3 tomatoes
- 2 avocados
- Shredded lettuce
- 4 pounds Russet potatoes
- 3 large eggs
- 1 bunch celery
- Diced pimiento
- Sweet pickle cubes
- ¾ cup sweetened flake coconut
- 12 navel oranges
- 1 pineapple

Check the Staples

- Butter
- Catsup
- Chili sauce
- Crackers
- Dijon mustard
- Dried parsley
- Garlic powder
- Ground thyme
- Hot sauce
- Mayonnaise
- Onion (1)
- Paprika
- Peppercorns
- Plain breadcrumbs
- Salt
- Worcestershire sauce
- Yellow mustard

Suggested Wines

There are loads of unique and interesting white wines that pair well with seafood. I find that almost any of the European wine regions bordering the Mediterranean produce white wines that work well with fish. Try some of the Italian whites: Gavi di Gavi, Lugana, or Greco di Tufo. Crisp, clean, and light in body, these wines taste great cold and are very refreshing. Plus, their fruit-forward personality balances spicy ingredients. Any of the New Zealand Sauvignon Blancs will also work well.

For red wine lovers, choose a nice Pinot Noir. Whether from the United States or France, these fruit-driven red wines work great for dishes that are lighter in flavor. —D.H.

Pecan Smoked Trout Spread

- Peel the skin from each trout fillet. Finely chop the trout. In a medium mixing bowl combine the trout with the cream cheese, sour cream, lemon juice, chopped dill, mustard, and hot sauce.
- Cover and chill for 1 hour. Transfer to a serving bowl and garnish with fresh dill if desired.
- Serve with crackers or toast points.

MAKES 2 CUPS

½ pound pecan smoked trout

1 8-ounce package cream cheese, softened

⅓ cup sour cream

Juice of 1 lemon

2 tablespoons chopped fresh dill

1 teaspoon Dijon mustard

¼ teaspoon hot sauce

Fresh dill for garnish, optional

HOT TIP

Smoked trout is available in most large grocery stores. It's usually in the same section as the smoked salmon. Pecan smoked trout has been cooked over pecan wood. If you can't find smoked trout, use smoked salmon.

LIVING LIGHT

⅓ less fat cream cheese (Neufchatel) can be used in place of regular cream cheese. Low-fat sour cream can be used as well.

Spicy Catfish Sandwiches

1 cup plain breadcrumbs

1 teaspoon salt

½ teaspoon freshly ground pepper

¼ teaspoon ground thyme

1 teaspoon dried parsley

¼ teaspoon garlic powder

4 6-ounce catfish fillets

½ cup butter, melted

1 16-ounce loaf French bread

Zesty Mayonnaise (see recipe at right)

3 tomatoes, thinly sliced

2 avocadoes, thinly sliced

Shredded lettuce

- Preheat the oven to 500°. Line a rimmed baking sheet with aluminum foil.
- In a shallow dish combine the breadcrumbs, salt, pepper, thyme, parsley, and garlic powder.
- Cut the fillets in half width-wise. Using a pastry brush lightly brush the fillets with melted butter. Coat the fillets with the breadcrumb mixture.
- Place the coated fillets on the prepared baking sheet and bake, uncovered, for 10 to 12 minutes or until the fillets flake easily with a fork.
- Allow the fillets to cool for 10 minutes before assembling the sandwiches.
- Cut the French bread loaf in half, creating a top and a bottom. Spread Zesty Mayonnaise on both cut sides of the bread.
- Place the catfish on the bottom half of the bread. Top with sliced tomatoes, sliced avocados, and shredded lettuce. Place the top half of the bread over the lettuce.
- The sandwich can be served sliced into 4 or 6 smaller sandwiches.

MAKES 4 TO 6 SERVINGS

Zesty Mayonnaise

- In a medium bowl whisk together the mayonnaise, chili sauce, catsup, pepper, Worcestershire sauce, mustard, hot sauce, and paprika.
- Cover and chill.

MAKES ABOUT 2¾ CUPS

2   cups mayonnaise

½   cup chili sauce

¼   cup catsup

2   teaspoons freshly ground pepper

1   tablespoon Worcestershire sauce

1   tablespoon yellow mustard

½   teaspoon hot sauce

⅛   teaspoon paprika

Old-Fashioned Potato Salad

4	pounds Russet potatoes, peeled and cut into 3-inch pieces
3	large eggs, hard-boiled and chopped
1	cup finely chopped celery
⅔	cup finely chopped onion
1	cup mayonnaise
⅔	cup sweet pickle cubes
¼	cup diced pimiento
1	teaspoon salt
½	teaspoon freshly ground pepper

- In a large stockpot cover the potatoes with cold water. Bring the water to a boil and cook until the potatoes are tender when tested with a fork, about 30 minutes.
- Drain the potatoes and place in a large mixing bowl. Using a potato masher gently mash the potatoes 3 to 4 times. Don't completely mash all of the potatoes.
- Add the eggs, celery, onion, mayonnaise, pickle cubes, pimiento, salt, and pepper. Stir to combine all ingredients.
- Refrigerate until ready to serve.

MAKES 8 TO 10 SERVINGS

LIVING LIGHT

Low-fat mayonnaise can be used in place of regular mayonnaise.

Pineapple and Orange Ambrosia

- In a large glass mixing bowl combine the pineapple and oranges.
- Stir in the coconut.
- Cover and chill overnight.

MAKES 8 TO 10 SERVINGS

1   fresh pineapple, cored and cut into ½-inch pieces (about 3½ cups)

12 navel oranges, peeled and cut into segments

¾   cup sweetened flake coconut

Hors d'Oeuvres for All

Tangy Pickled Shrimp
Tomato and Kalamata Bruschetta
Seared Beef Tenderloin with Creamy Horseradish Sauce
Bakery Rolls
Cheddar Cheese Straws
Water
Beer
Soft Drinks
Recommended Wines, if desired

Hors d'Oeuvres for All

This versatile menu fits so many occasions. It's great for holiday entertaining, a couples baby shower, or even a family gathering. I love to "graze" on good appetizers, and this menu makes that possible for everyone. Once your guests see the gorgeous beef tenderloin sliced on a platter, they'll be dying to get in line for the food.

You'll want to have a stack of salad plates from your cabinet or small very nice paper plates. With the great food selection, the guests will go back for seconds, and they'll want plates to pile the food on. Thank goodness hors d'oeuvres don't have to be dainty anymore!

TIMELINE

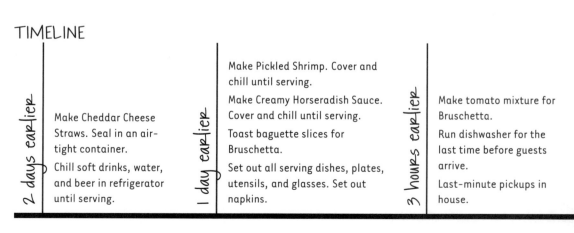

2 days earlier

Make Cheddar Cheese Straws. Seal in an air-tight container.

Chill soft drinks, water, and beer in refrigerator until serving.

1 day earlier

Make Pickled Shrimp. Cover and chill until serving.

Make Creamy Horseradish Sauce. Cover and chill until serving.

Toast baguette slices for Bruschetta.

Set out all serving dishes, plates, utensils, and glasses. Set out napkins.

3 hours earlier

Make tomato mixture for Bruschetta.

Run dishwasher for the last time before guests arrive.

Last-minute pickups in house.

Serving Suggestions

Tangy Pickled Shrimp

I like to serve these "can't have just one" appetizers in a big serving bowl with a slotted spoon. Place a small plate with decorative toothpicks beside the serving bowl to make the shrimp a little less messy on the hands.

Tomato and Kalamata Bruschetta

If you have stackable clear cake stands, this is the time to use them. If you don't have a set of cake stands, go for a large platter that gives plenty of room for the bruschetta. You don't want them to overlap.

Seared Beef Tenderloin with Creamy Horseradish Sauce

A large shallow platter is perfect for the star of the party. Place a pair of tongs or a serving fork with the beef for easy pickup. You'll want to put the Creamy Horseradish Sauce in a small serving bowl with a small spoon.

Bakery Rolls

Place the rolls beside the beef in a basket covered in a large napkin or linen towel.

Cheddar Cheese Straws

There are several ways to serve Cheddar Cheese Straws. Standing them upright in clear glasses or mint julep cups makes a fun presentation. You can also stack them on small plates or serve them on a wooden board as you would fresh cheese.

You'll Need . . .

2 medium mixing bowls

Large nonreactive mixing bowl

Medium nonreactive mixing bowl

Pastry brush

Coffee grinder or mortar and pestle

14-inch skillet or roasting pan, or griddle

Rimmed baking sheet

Food processor

Rolling pin

Pizza cutter or large knife

Baking sheet

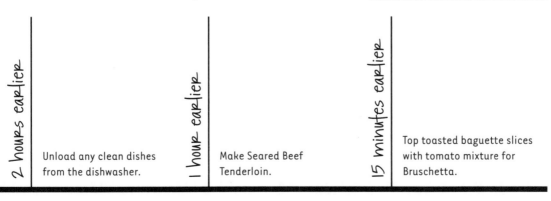

2 hours earlier — Unload any clean dishes from the dishwasher.

1 hour earlier — Make Seared Beef Tenderloin.

15 minutes earlier — Top toasted baguette slices with tomato mixture for Bruschetta.

Grocery List

- 1 4½-pound beef tenderloin
- ¼ cup whipping cream
- 2½ pounds tomatoes
- 2 lemons
- Fresh parsley
- Kalamata olives
- 2 baguettes
- 8 ounces extra-sharp Cheddar cheese
- Green peppercorns
- 2 pounds cooked shrimp
- Capers
- Bakery rolls

Check the Staples

- All-purpose flour
- Baking powder
- Butter
- Cayenne pepper
- Celery seed
- Dijon mustard
- Garlic
- Kosher salt
- Mayonnaise
- Olive oil
- Onion (1)
- Peppercorns
- Prepared horseradish
- Salt
- Sugar
- Sweet onion (1)
- Vegetable oil
- White balsamic vinegar
- White wine vinegar

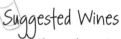

Suggested Wines

When choosing wines for a party or group of people, try to stick to ones that will please many palates. This means to stay away from wines that are bold in flavor or very rich. Good white wine choices include French Chardonnay (it's lighter in body and less oaky than California and Australia). For something different, try a white from Greece or a dry Riesling from Germany.

My all-time favorite red wine for parties is French Beaujolais. Made from the Gamay grape, Beaujolais is a light, fruity, refreshing wine that pairs well with a variety of foods. —D.H.

Tangy Pickled Shrimp

- In a medium mixing bowl combine the vegetable oil, the vinegars, green peppercorns, salt, pepper, sugar, lemon juice, lemon zest, capers, cayenne pepper, and celery seed.
- In a large nonreactive mixing bowl combine the shrimp and onion. Pour the vegetable oil mixture over the shrimp and toss well. Cover tightly and chill for at least 8 hours.
- Can be served over lettuce or alone.

MAKES 8 TO 10 SERVINGS

⅓ cup vegetable oil

½ cup white wine vinegar

¼ cup white balsamic vinegar

1 tablespoon green peppercorns, drained

½ teaspoon salt

⅛ teaspoon freshly ground pepper

1 tablespoon sugar

1 teaspoon lemon juice

1 teaspoon lemon zest

1 tablespoon capers, drained

¼ teaspoon cayenne pepper

¾ teaspoon celery seed

2 pounds cooked peeled shrimp, tails on

1 medium sweet onion, thinly sliced

HOT TIPS

Look for green peppercorns in the olive and pickle section of the grocery store. They are packed in brine and bottled in small jars.

I like to buy cooked peeled shrimp from the seafood market to save myself the hassle of cooking my own.

White balsamic vinegar adds all the flavor of traditional balsamic vinegar without the dark color.

Tomato and Kalamata Bruschetta

2½ pounds fresh ripe
    tomatoes, seeded and
    chopped

½   cup finely diced onion

1   garlic clove, minced

1   tablespoon olive oil

2   teaspoons fresh lemon
    juice

2   tablespoons chopped fresh
    parsley

½   teaspoon salt

¼   teaspoon freshly ground
    pepper

10 Kalamata olives, pitted
    and chopped

2   baguettes, sliced into
    ¼-inch slices

½   cup olive oil

- In a medium nonreactive mixing bowl combine the tomatoes, onion, garlic, olive oil, lemon juice, parsley, salt, and pepper. Stir in the chopped olives.
- Brush the bread slices with olive oil. Broil on each side until lightly browned. Allow to cool.
- Top each toasted bread slice with 1 tablespoon tomato mixture. Serve immediately.

MAKES ABOUT 4 DOZEN

Seared Beef Tenderloin with Creamy Horseradish Sauce

- In a medium mixing bowl whisk together the mayonnaise, cream, mustard, and horseradish. Add more horseradish if desired. Add salt and pepper to taste. Cover and refrigerate until ready to serve.
- Using a coffee grinder or a mortar and pestle, grind the peppercorns until coarsely ground. Add the kosher salt to the ground pepper. Rub the tenderloin with olive oil until coated. Rub the pepper mixture over the tenderloin until generously coated.
- In a 14-inch skillet or a roasting pan or griddle heat 3 tablespoons of olive oil over medium-high heat. Add the tenderloin and cook on each side just until browned.
- Transfer the tenderloin to a rimmed baking sheet and bake at 350° until the meat reaches 140° (medium-rare), about 30 minutes. (Some enjoy beef tenderloin rather rare. Remove from the oven at 130° if you like it less cooked.) Allow the meat to sit for 10 minutes before slicing.
- Serve sliced tenderloin and Creamy Horseradish Sauce with bakery rolls.

1	cup mayonnaise
¼	cup whipping cream
1	tablespoon Dijon mustard
¼	cup prepared horseradish, or more if desired
	Salt and freshly ground pepper to taste
¼	cup peppercorns
3	tablespoons kosher salt
1	4½-pound beef tenderloin, trimmed and tied
	Olive oil
	Bakery rolls

MAKES 15 SERVINGS

HOT TIPS

Asking your butcher to trim and tie your tenderloin will save time. Trimming a tenderloin entails removing the silver skin and the excess fat. Tying simply ensures that the meat is the same thickness throughout for even cooking.

Buy a separate coffee grinder for grinding spices. I have a white one for coffee and a black one for spices so I won't forget which one to use. It's an easy way to grind and crush dried spices and herbs.

LIVING LIGHT

Low-fat mayonnaise can be used in place of regular mayonnaise.

Cheddar Cheese Straws

8　ounces extra-sharp
　　Cheddar cheese, shredded
½　cup butter, softened
1¾　cups all-purpose flour
2　teaspoons baking powder
½　teaspoon cayenne pepper

- Preheat oven to 400°.
- In a food processor process the Cheddar cheese and butter until creamy.
- In a medium bowl combine the flour, baking powder, and cayenne pepper. Add the dry ingredients to the cheese mixture in the food processor.
- Pulse until the dough comes together in a ball.
- Place the dough on a lightly floured surface and roll into a 7 x 11-inch rectangle.
- Using a pizza cutter, slice the dough in half lengthwise. Make 20 horizontal cuts (making each cheese straw approximately 3½ x ½-inch).
- Gently move the cheese straws to an ungreased baking sheet. Bake at 400° for 10 to 12 minutes or until crisp and lightly browned on the bottom. Allow to cool completely on a cooling rack.

MAKES ABOUT 80

HOT
TIPS

Pre-shredded cheese has a lower moisture content than blocks of cheese. I find I get better results in baking when I grate my own.

Gather for Grilling

Red Potato Salad with Thyme Vinaigrette

Summer Grilled Vegetables

Rosemary Mustard Pork Tenderloin

Citrus Delight Ice Cream

Sweet Tea

Water with Lemon

Recommended Wines, if desired

Gather for Grilling

I just love when the weather warms up enough to dust off the grill and cook outdoors. Down here in the South, it's quite a bonus if you can have a hot meal and not have to heat up the kitchen. It's usually hot enough without turning on the oven. Plus, the taste of the charcoal on grilled foods just can't be beat.

Feel free to serve this menu right outside on the porch. That way you can grill when your guests arrive and still spend time with them. Once the pork hits the grill, the rosemary aroma keeps the guests from straying too far.

TIMELINE

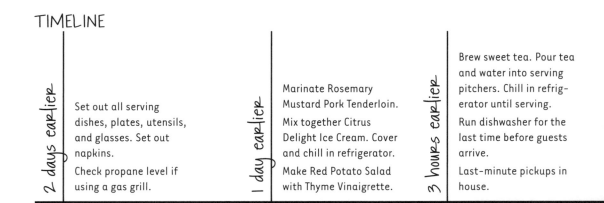

2 days earlier

Set out all serving dishes, plates, utensils, and glasses. Set out napkins.

Check propane level if using a gas grill.

1 day earlier

Marinate Rosemary Mustard Pork Tenderloin.

Mix together Citrus Delight Ice Cream. Cover and chill in refrigerator.

Make Red Potato Salad with Thyme Vinaigrette.

3 hours earlier

Brew sweet tea. Pour tea and water into serving pitchers. Chill in refrigerator until serving.

Run dishwasher for the last time before guests arrive.

Last-minute pickups in house.

Serving Suggestions

Red Potato Salad with Thyme Vinaigrette
A serving bowl is really the only way to go for a big batch of potato salad. If it's just not possible, use a deep platter.

Summer Grilled Vegetables
A large platter or shallow bowl will work nicely for this colorful side dish. The more you can show off the colors, the better.

Rosemary Mustard Pork Tenderloin
Serve the two pork tenderloins on a wooden carving board. Make sure it has ridges to catch the juices. A small platter is also a nice serving piece for the meat.

Citrus Delight Ice Cream
I like to chill bowls ahead of time in the freezer and serve individual dishes of the ice cream. When guests are eating homemade ice cream, they usually don't notice the serving dish! It melts quickly, so work fast.

You'll Need . . .

Stockpot

Small mixing bowl

Colander

2 large mixing bowls

Grill basket or heavy-duty aluminum foil

Large zippered plastic bag

Grill (gas or charcoal)

Meat thermometer

Ice cream maker

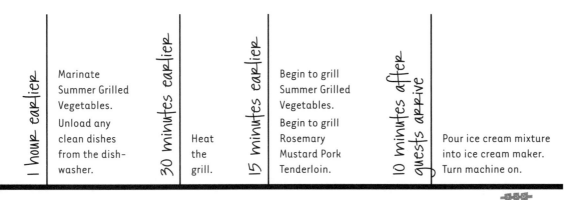

1 hour earlier
Marinate Summer Grilled Vegetables.
Unload any clean dishes from the dishwasher.

30 minutes earlier
Heat the grill.

15 minutes earlier
Begin to grill Summer Grilled Vegetables.
Begin to grill Rosemary Mustard Pork Tenderloin.

10 minutes after guests arrive
Pour ice cream mixture into ice cream maker. Turn machine on.

Grocery List

- 2 1-pound pork tenderloins
- 1½ pounds red potatoes
- 1 lemon
- 1 bunch fresh thyme
- 1 bunch fresh parsley, optional
- 8 ounces button mushrooms
- 2 yellow squash
- 1 red bell pepper
- 1 pound fresh asparagus
- 1½ cups milk
- 2 cups whipping cream
- ¾ cup half and half
- 2 oranges
- 3 limes
- Fresh rosemary

Check the Staples

- Dijon mustard
- Dried basil
- Dried oregano
- Garlic
- Honey
- Olive oil
- Onion (1)
- Peppercorns
- Red wine vinegar
- Salt
- Sugar
- White balsamic vinegar
- Whole grained mustard

Suggested Wines

When it comes to pork, I have one overwhelming favorite—Pinot Noir. While I prefer the richer, earthier ones from France's Burgundy region, especially the Côte de Nuits, Oregon and parts of the Sonoma Valley in California are making excellent Pinot Noir. New Zealand is also producing some interesting wines made from Pinot Noir.

A lighter-style Chianti is another excellent choice. —D.H.

Southern Entertaining for a New Generation

Red Potato Salad with Thyme Vinaigrette

- Cut the potatoes into 1-inch pieces.
- In a stockpot cover the potatoes with water and bring to a boil. Boil for 10 minutes or until the potatoes are tender when tested with a fork.
- In a small bowl whisk together the vinegar, mustard, garlic, lemon juice, thyme, salt, and pepper. While whisking, slowly pour the olive oil into the vinegar mixture.
- Drain the potatoes using a colander and place in a large serving bowl. Add dressing and toss lightly, being careful not to tear the potatoes. Garnish with fresh parsley if desired.

MAKES 6 SERVINGS

1½ pounds small red potatoes
2 tablespoons red wine vinegar
½ teaspoon Dijon mustard
1 clove garlic, minced
½ tablespoon lemon juice
1 tablespoon fresh thyme or ½ teaspoon ground thyme
¾ teaspoon salt
¼ teaspoon freshly ground pepper
¼ cup olive oil
Chopped fresh parsley for garnish, optional

HOT TIP

Buy the smallest red potatoes you can find. They tend to be more tender.

Summer Grilled Vegetables

⅓ cup white balsamic vinegar

¼ cup olive oil

1 teaspoon honey

2 garlic cloves, minced

½ teaspoon dried oregano

½ teaspoon dried basil

½ teaspoon salt

¼ teaspoon pepper

8 ounces fresh button mushrooms, stems removed and caps halved

2 yellow squash, cut into ½-inch thick slices

1 red bell pepper, cut into 1-inch pieces

1 onion, cut into 1-inch pieces

1 pound fresh asparagus

- In a large mixing bowl whisk together the vinegar, olive oil, and honey until blended.
- Add the garlic, oregano, basil, salt, and pepper.
- Add the vegetables to the marinade, tossing to coat all pieces. Let stand for 45 minutes.
- Place the vegetables in a grill basket (see below). Discard the marinade. Grill on medium-low heat for 6 to 7 minutes. Flip the basket and grill for 5 more minutes or until the pieces are slightly charred.

MAKES 6 SERVINGS

HOT TIP

If you don't have a grill basket, make a "basket" out of heavy-duty aluminum foil. Grill in the foil and just stir the vegetables every few minutes.

Rosemary Mustard Pork Tenderloin

- Trim the fat and silver skin from the tenderloins. Set aside.
- In a large zippered plastic bag combine the olive oil, mustards, rosemary, garlic, salt, and pepper. Add the pork to the bag, seal, and toss to coat.
- Marinate in the refrigerator for at least 1 hour or overnight.
- Grill over medium-hot coals for 20 to 25 minutes, turning occasionally, or until a meat thermometer reads 150°.
- Let the tenderloins rest for 10 minutes before slicing.
- Slice the tenderloins into ½-inch pieces to serve.
- Garnish with fresh rosemary, if desired.

MAKES 6 SERVINGS

2   1-pound pork tenderloins
¼   cup olive oil
2   tablespoons whole-grained mustard
2   tablespoons Dijon mustard
1   tablespoon chopped fresh rosemary
2   garlic cloves, minced
¾   teaspoon salt
½   teaspoon freshly ground pepper
     Fresh rosemary for garnish, optional

Citrus Delight Ice Cream

1½ cups milk

2 cups heavy whipping cream

¾ cup half and half

1½ cups sugar

2 tablespoons lime zest

2 tablespoons orange zest

¼ cup fresh lime juice

¼ cup fresh orange juice

- In a large mixing bowl whisk together the milk, cream, half and half, sugar, lime zest, orange zest, lime juice, and orange juice.
- Pour the mixture into the freezer container of a half-gallon ice cream maker. Freeze according to manufacturer's instructions.

MAKES ½ GALLON

HOT TIPS

Another standard size for ice cream makers is 1 gallon. Double the recipe if your freezer is a 1-gallon machine.

Because this recipe doesn't have eggs, it's safe for everyone to try.

Dessert Party

Banana Pudding
Tom's 1-2-3-4 Cake
Tom's Caramel Icing
Chocolate Fondue with Strawberries
Meringue Kisses
Decaffeinated Coffee
Milk
Recommended Wines, if desired

Dessert Party

Who doesn't like to stay up late and eat sweet treats? I certainly do. This menu is excellent for celebrations of any kind. Add a bottle of champagne and toast the occasion. Try hosting this party that has a little different concept. Have your friends come over at 8:00 or 9:00 at night for dessert. It's a great way to top off an evening out. Best of all, the recipes are all make ahead, so you can go out too.

I can't guarantee that you'll be able to sleep after all the sugar, but it's worth losing a little shuteye for. If it's warm outside, try serving iced decaf coffee and chocolate milk.

TIMELINE

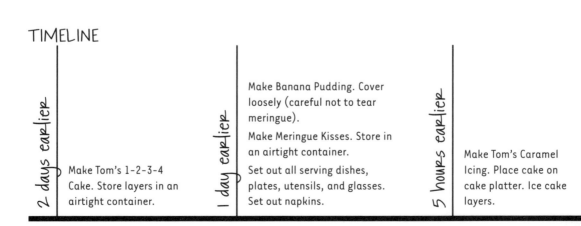

2 days earlier
Make Tom's 1-2-3-4 Cake. Store layers in an airtight container.

1 day earlier
Make Banana Pudding. Cover loosely (careful not to tear meringue).

Make Meringue Kisses. Store in an airtight container.

Set out all serving dishes, plates, utensils, and glasses. Set out napkins.

5 hours earlier
Make Tom's Caramel Icing. Place cake on cake platter. Ice cake layers.

Banana Pudding

Your pudding will need to be served in the 8 x 8-inch baking dish that you baked it in. It's prettiest before it's cut, so set it on the buffet before you decide to dig in.

Tom's 1-2-3-4 Cake and Tom's Caramel Icing

A beautiful cake covered in home-made icing is only fitting on a cake platter or a cake plate. Don't forget to set out your cake/pie server.

Chocolate Fondue with Strawberries

A fondue pot is perfect for keeping the chocolate warm for dipping. Pile the strawberries high on a platter. I like a white platter because it really shows off the red strawberries.

Meringue Kisses

Stack these crunchy delights in a basket or a bowl.

You'll Need . . .

2 large heavy saucepans
Small mixing bowl
Electric mixer
8 x 8-inch casserole dish
3 8-inch cake pans
Parchment paper
Large mixing bowl
Flour sifter or wire-mesh sieve
Medium mixing bowl
Medium, heavy saucepan
Cooling racks
Fondue pot and forks
Rimmed baking sheet

---

3 hours earlier
Run dishwasher for the last time before guests arrive.
Make Chocolate Fondue. Cover and set aside until reheating.
Last-minute pick-ups in house.

2 hours earlier
Unload any clean dishes from the dishwasher.

1 hour earlier
Brew coffee.

30 minutes earlier
Wash strawberries.

15 minutes earlier
Reheat Chocolate Fondue on low heat.

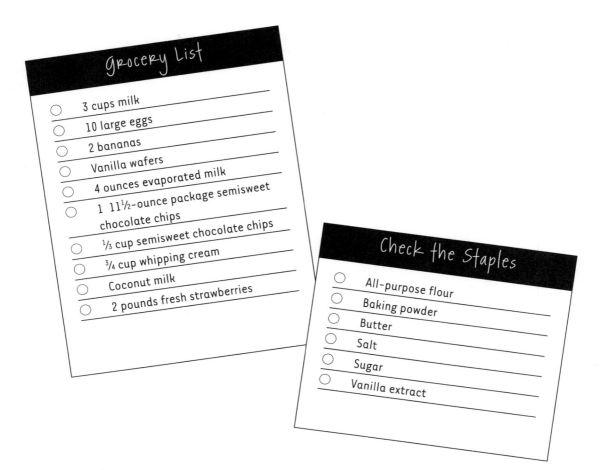

Grocery List

- 3 cups milk
- 10 large eggs
- 2 bananas
- Vanilla wafers
- 4 ounces evaporated milk
- 1 11½-ounce package semisweet chocolate chips
- ⅓ cup semisweet chocolate chips
- ¾ cup whipping cream
- Coconut milk
- 2 pounds fresh strawberries

Check the Staples

- All-purpose flour
- Baking powder
- Butter
- Salt
- Sugar
- Vanilla extract

Suggested Wines

When it comes to pairing wine with dessert, remember one thing: less is more. It's easy to go overboard on the sweetness. For lighter desserts that rely on vanilla for flavor, I like Sauternes. When it comes to fruit desserts, try a sweet German Riesling. Australia and New Zealand also make some excellent and very affordable dessert wines. Chocolate desserts are divine with an Italian Brachetto. Brachetto is a red, sparkling dessert wine that pairs absolutely perfectly with chocolate. It may take some time to find, but it is worth the effort. —D.H.

Banana Pudding

- Preheat the oven to 400°.
- In a large, heavy saucepan combine the sugar, salt, and flour. Whisk in the milk. Bring the mixture to a boil over medium heat, whisking constantly. Remove from the heat.
- In a small mixing bowl whisk the egg yolks until pale yellow and creamy. Gradually add a small amount of the hot milk mixture to the egg yolks, whisking constantly, then slowly add the egg yolk mixture to the hot milk mixture, whisking constantly. Stir in the vanilla extract.
- Using an electic mixer beat the egg whites until soft peaks form. Continue beating, adding the sugar 1 tablespoon at a time. Beat until stiff peaks form.
- Place the sliced bananas in the bottom of an 8 x 8-inch casserole dish. Cover the bananas with vanilla wafers. Pour the custard mixture over the vanilla wafers.
- Spread the meringue over the custard mixture, using a knife to create curls and peaks.
- Bake at 400° for 12 to 13 minutes or until lightly browned.
- Chill for at least 3 hours before serving.

MAKES 8 SERVINGS

½	cup sugar
1	teaspoon salt
⅓	cup all-purpose flour
2	cups milk
1	teaspoon vanilla extract
4	large eggs, separated
½	cup sugar
2	large bananas, cut into ¼-inch slices
3	cups vanilla wafers

Tom's 1-2-3-4 Cake

1 cup butter, softened
2 cups sugar
4 large eggs, separated
1 teaspoon vanilla extract
¼ teaspoon salt
3 cups all-purpose flour
3 teaspoons baking powder
1 cup milk

- Preheat the oven to 350°. Grease and flour three 8-inch cake pans. Line the bottom of the pans with parchment paper.
- In a large mixing bowl cream the butter and sugar using an electric mixer for 2 minutes. Add the egg yolks, one at a time. Add the vanilla extract.
- In a medium bowl sift the salt, flour, and baking powder together. Add to the butter mixture alternately with the milk, beginning and ending with the flour mixture.
- Beat the egg whites until soft peaks form. Fold the egg whites into the batter using a large spoon or spatula.
- Pour the batter into the prepared cake pans.
- Bake at 350° for 15 to 18 minutes or until a wooden pick inserted into the middle of the cakes comes out clean.
- Allow the cakes to cool in the pans for 5 minutes.
- Remove from the pans and cool completely on cooling racks. Frost with Tom's Caramel Icing (see recipe at right) or desired icing.

MAKES 10 TO 12 SERVINGS

HOT TIPS

Baking powder and baking soda have expiration dates. Both products are only good for about a year.

FUN FACTS

Why "1-2-3-4"? Take a look at the amounts for the ingredients.

This recipe has been in my family for generations. My grandmother told me she first learned this recipe when she was married in 1942.

Tom's Caramel Icing

- In a medium, heavy saucepan combine the sugar and evaporated milk. Bring to a simmer over medium heat, stirring constantly until all of the sugar is dissolved.
- Bring to a rolling boil over medium heat. Boil for 4 minutes. Reduce the heat to low and cook for 1 minute 30 seconds.
- Remove from the heat and carefully stir in the vanilla extract and butter. Stir constantly until the butter is melted.
- Let the icing cool for 5 minutes before spreading on the cooled cake layers. The icing will be thin. Spoon about ⅓ cup icing in between layers and the rest over the top of the cake. A spatula may be needed to thoroughly cover the sides of the cake. The icing will set as it cools on the cake.

2 cups sugar
1 4-ounce can evaporated milk
1 teaspoon vanilla extract
½ cup butter

Chocolate Fondue with Strawberries

1   11½-ounce package
    semisweet chocolate chips

¾   cup whipping cream

½   cup coconut milk

½   teaspoon vanilla extract

2   pounds fresh strawberries

- In a large, heavy saucepan combine the chocolate chips and cream. Stirring constantly, melt the chocolate chips on low heat.
- Once the chocolate is melted, add the coconut milk and vanilla extract, whisking to combine.
- Place the chocolate in a fondue pot over a low flame or a small candle.
- To serve, dip the strawberries in the chocolate.

MAKES 8 SERVINGS

HOT TIPS

Chocolate fondue can be made up to 6 hours in advance and covered at room temperature. Reheat on low heat.

Meringue Kisses

- Preheat the oven to 250°. Line a rimmed baking sheet with parchment paper.
- In a medium bowl beat the egg whites using an electric mixer until stiff peaks form. Gradually add the salt and sugar, 1 teaspoon at a time, until all of the sugar is dissolved.
- Add the vanilla extract. Stir in the chocolate chips.
- Using a teaspoon, drop the meringues onto the parchment paper, allowing 1 inch in between.
- Bake at 400° for 1 hour or until completely hardened and light to the touch. Break one kiss open to ensure they are completely dry on the inside before taking out of the oven.

MAKES ABOUT 36

2   egg whites
     Pinch of salt
½   cup granulated sugar
½   teaspoon vanilla extract
⅓   cup semisweet chocolate chips

Helpful Conversions

½ tablespoon..1½ teaspoons

1 tablespoon ....3 teaspoons

2 tablespoons ....⅛ cup

3 tablespoons ....1 jigger

4 tablespoons ....¼ cup

5 tablespoons plus 1 teaspoon ....⅓ cup

8 tablespoons ....½ cup

10 tablespoons plus 2 teaspoons ....⅔ cup

12 tablespoons ....¾ cup

16 tablespoons ....1 cup

2 cups ....1 pint

2 pints ....1 quart

4 quarts ....1 gallon

4 ounces ....¼ pound

8 ounces ....½ pound

16 ounces ....1 pound

1 tablespoon ....½ fluid ounce

2 tablespoons ....1 fluid ounce

¼ cup ....2 liquid ounces

½ cup ....4 liquid ounces

¾ cup ....6 liquid ounces

1 cup ....8 liquid ounces

2 cups..1 pint................................16 liquid ounces

3 cups		24 liquid ounces
4 cups	1 quart	32 liquid ounces
8 cups	½ gallon	64 liquid ounces
16 cups	1 gallon	128 liquid ounces

Questioning your pan size? Check on the bottom of the pan for a size. If you don't see one, pull out your ruler to measure the bottom of the pan, or fill the pan with water to measure its volume.

8 x 8-inch pan	8 cups
9 x 13-inch pan	13 cups to 15 cups
8-inch round cake pan	5 cups
4-ounce ramekins	½ cup

Southern Substitutions

No one wants to have to run to the grocery store every time they run out of an ingredient in the middle of a recipe. Knowing some basic substitutions may save you an extra trip.

1 cup buttermilk .... 1 cup milk plus 1 tablespoon white vinegar

1 cup self-rising flour .... 1 cup all-purpose flour plus ½ teaspoon salt plus 1 teaspoon baking powder

1 cup corn syrup .... 1 cup honey

1 tablespoon fresh herbs .... 1 teaspoon dried herbs

1 tablespoon fresh rosemary .... 1 tablespoon dried rosemary (exception to above rule)

1 vanilla bean .... 1 tablespoon vanilla extract

1 vanilla bean .... 1 tablespoon vanilla bean paste

1 clove garlic .... ⅛ teaspoon garlic powder

1 tablespoon chopped shallots .... 2 teaspoons chopped onion plus 1 small minced garlic clove

1 cup brown sugar .... 1 cup granulated sugar

1 tablespoon cornstarch .... 2 teaspoons arrowroot

1 tablespoon cornstarch .... 2 tablespoons all-purpose flour

1 stick butter .... 1 stick margarine; do not substitute with whipped or low-fat margarine due to the differences in moisture content

Guide to the Recipes and Sources for Ingredients

- All ingredients are regular, not low-fat or fat-free, unless stated in the recipe. Light ingredients are listed only when the recipe won't be comprised by using them.

- Butter: All butter is unsalted butter.

- Shortening: I use Crisco shortening.

- Flour: I only use White Lily Flour (self-rising and all-purpose). This flour is readily available throughout the Southeast. To find or order White Lily Flour, call 1-800-264-5459. Flour is measured by spooning into a dry measuring cup then leveling off with the flat edge of a knife.

- Salt: All salt is iodized table salt, unless otherwise stated.

- Hot Sauce: Green Pepper Tabasco is used for all hot sauce needs.

- White Truffle Oil: To order, contact The Cook's Warehouse at 1-800-499-0996 or visit www.cookswarehouse.com.

- Vanilla Bean Paste: To order, contact The Cook's Warehouse.

Index

a

ambrosia, pineapple and orange, 145, 151
Anything Goes Cobb Salad, 85, 88
Apricot Puffs, 75, 81
artichoke hearts, 135
asparagus
    Summer Grilled Vegetables, 166
asparagus, herb-roasted, 133, 136
avocados
    Anything Goes Cobb Salad, 88
    Spicy Catfish Sandwiches, 148

b

Baby Spinach with Tomatoes and Onions, 67, 71
bacon
    Charleston Shrimp and Creamy Grits, 32–33
    Fried Green Tomatoes with Goat Cheese and Bacon, 95
    Sweet Balsamic Bacon, 41
Bacon Deviled Eggs, 113, 115

Balsamic Strawberries, 29, 34
Balsamic Vinaigrette, 138
balsamic vinegar
    Herb-Roasted Asparagus, 136
    Summer Grilled Vegetables, 166
    Sweet Balsamic Bacon, 41
    Tangy Pickled Shrimp, 157
Banana Pudding, 171, 173
Banana–White Chocolate Muffins, 47, 51
beef tenderloin, seared, 159
Bellinis, 123, 128
Bibb lettuce, 108
biscuits, 29, 31
Black-and-White Chocolate Mint Brownies, 133, 139
blackberries
    Buttermilk Panna Cotta, 110
    Very Berry Tart, 99
blueberries
    Very Berry Tart, 99
    Very Blueberry Muffins, 50
Boiled Peanuts, 113, 119
Bourbon Walnut Coffee Cake, 57, 59
Breakfast Smoothies, 47, 49

Fried Chicken, 75, 79
Fried Green Tomatoes with Goat
    Cheese and Bacon, 93, 95
fried pies. *See* Apricot Puffs

g

Georgia Pimiento Cheese, 113, 117
gingersnaps, 116
goat cheese and bacon, fried green
    tomatoes with, 93, 95
Green Beans with Lemon, 75, 80
grilled vegetables, summer, 163, 166
grits, 32–33

h

Herb-Crusted Racks of Lamb, 67, 70
Herb-Roasted Asparagus, 133, 136
Herbed Egg Salad Lettuce Rolls, 105,
    108
Homemade Limeade, 93, 98
honey, toasted pecan cinnamon, 39, 44
horseradish sauce, creamy, 155, 159
hot chocolate, rich, 57, 62

i

ice cream
    Citrus Delight Ice Cream, 168
    Cool Pumpkin Squares, 116

k

Kalamata olives, 158
Key Lime Tartlets, 105, 109
kiwis, 110

l

lamb, herb-crusted racks of, 67, 70
lemon, green beans with, 75, 80
lettuce rolls, egg salad, 105, 108

m

macaroni and cheese, Sa's, 75, 77
Mamie's Sugar Cookies, 85, 90
Mango Margaritas, 123, 127
mayonnaise
    Old-Fashioned Potato Salad, 150
    Seared Beef Tenderoin with Creamy
        Horseradish Sauce, 159
    Zesty Mayonnaise, 149
Meringue Kisses, 171, 177
mimosas, Southern, 29, 35
Mini Cucumber Sandwiches, 105, 107
Miss Tom's Basic Biscuits, 29, 31
Mojitos, 123, 126
Mom's Squash Casserole, 75, 78
muffins
    Banana–White Chocolate Muffins,
        51
    Very Blueberry Muffins, 50

mushrooms, 166

O

Old-Fashioned Potato Salad, 145, 150
onions
    Baby Spinach with Tomatoes and
      Onions, 71
    Pickled Cucumbers and Vidalias, 118
    Summer Grilled Vegetables, 166
oranges, 151

P

panna cotta, buttermilk, 105, 110
peaches
    Bellinis, 128
    Peach Butter, 53
peanut brittle, sweet and spicy, 123,
    129
peanuts, boiled, 113, 119
pears, white wine poached, 57, 61
Pecan Smoked Trout Spread, 145, 147
pecans
    Spinach Salad with Toasted Pecans,
      137
    Toasted Pecan Cinnamon Honey, 44

peppermint extract, 139
Pickled Cucumbers and Vidalias, 113,
    118
pimiento
    Georgia Pimiento Cheese, 117
    Old-Fashioned Potato Salad, 150
pineapple, 49, 151
Pineapple and Orange Ambrosia, 145,
    151
pork tenderloin, rosemary mustard,
    163, 167
potatoes
    Old-Fashioned Potato Salad, 150
    Red Potato Salad with Thyme
      Vinaigrette, 165
    Smashed Creamy Potatoes, 69
Pulled Chicken Salad Sandwiches, 85,
    89
pumpkin squares, cool, 113, 116

R

racks of lamb, herb-crusted, 67, 70
raspberries
    Buttermilk Panna Cotta, 110
    Very Berry Tart, 93, 99
Raspberry Butter, 47, 52
red bell pepper, 166
Red Potato Salad with Thyme
    Vinaigrette, 163, 165
Red Velvet Cake, 67, 72
Rich Hot Chocolate, 57, 62
Rosemary Mustard Pork Tenderloin,
    163, 167

About the Author

Rebecca Lang learned to cook from her grandmothers, both of whom were wonderful Southern cooks. Her formal training in culinary arts was at Johnson & Wales University. She has apprenticed with Nathalie Dupree and has been an assistant food editor and recipe developer for Oxmoor House. She is a food columnist for several newspapers throughout Georgia and Florida as well as a private cooking instructor and professional speaker. A graduate of the University of Georgia, she lives with her husband, Kevin, in Atlanta, Georgia.